Rana Bose

The Death of Abbie Hoffman and Other Plays

The Death of Abbie Hoffman and Other Plays

Rana Bose

With an introduction by
Uma Parameswaran

Seagull Books
CALCUTTA 1999

Cover photograph courtesy the author
Cover design: Naveen Kishore

ISBN 81 7046 153 7

*Published by Naveen Kishore, Seagull Books Private Limited,
26 Circus Avenue, Calcutta 700 017, India*

*Printed in India by A. Dasgupta at Sun Lithographing Co.
18, Hem Chandra Naskar Road, Calcutta 700 010, India*

Contents

Montreal Serai Theatre Group: A Note vi

An Author in Search of an Audience
Uma Parameswaran vii

Theatre Notes on a Bright October Morning in Montreal
Rana Bose xi

On the Double 1

The Death of Abbie Hoffman 21

The Sulpician Escarpment 57

Appendix:
'What politicized me was the power of performance'
An interview by Uma Parameswaran 103

Montreal Serai Theatre Group

Montreal Serai is an eleven-year-old theatre group that is committed to the creation of contemporary and innovative theatre, based in a newly interactive and intercultural Montreal. Montreal Serai reflects the linguistic, cultural, ethnic and political spectrum of this city. Disassociating itself from the traditional multicultural or purely ethnic theatre, the group strives to address the mainstream concerns of the peoples of this society, without necessarily adopting mainstream approaches. In this sense, Serai's theatre, language, music and cultural style reflect the urge to create and define a new interculturalism.

Both creation and performance of original theatre pieces have been undertaken. Although staging plays by other playwrights, emphasis has been laid on the creation of original plays reflecting the overall objectives of the group. In the past eleven years, nine plays by one of its members—Rana Bose—have been staged in Montreal and across Canada, including the highly successful *Baba Jacques Dass and Turmoil at Cote-des-Neiges Cemetery*, which played at the Centaur Theatre. More recent productions include *Nobody Gets Laid, The Death of Abbie Hoffman, Five or Six Characters in Search of Toronto* and *The Sulpician Escarpment.*

The strength of Montreal Serai lies in the diversity of the talents of its members and in their love for theatre. An intrinsic aspect of the theatre of the troupe has been its experimentation with contemporary issues in an avante-garde format. Raising issues of a significant political nature in an absolutely entertaining and effective manner, while combining 'homegrown' (low cost) technology, the group stages productions that are highly technical, from the point of view of stagecraft.

An Author in Search of an Audience

Born and schooled in Calcutta, with an engineering degree from Washington University in the United States, Rana Bose is now a dynamic playwright based in Montreal, Canada. He is also a senior executive with an engineering company, and his work takes him travelling to various countries, including India, which he has been visiting at least once a year during the last few years.

He has written and produced ten plays since 1986. The list includes: *Prairie Fire* (1977), *On the Double* (1986), *Baba Jacques Dass and Turmoil at Cote-des-Neiges Cemetery* (1987), *Some Dogs* (1988), *Who to Please?* (1989), *Nobody gets Laid* (1990), *The Death of Abbie Hoffman* (1991), *Five or Six Characters in Search of Toronto* (1993), *The Sulpician Escarpment* (1995) and *Blackskirt* (1998)

Rana Bose is the founding-director of Montreal Serai. Montreal Serai (Le Groupe Culturel Montreal Serai) has two wings. It is a theatre group that workshops and produces an average of a play each year; it is also a magazine that is published ten times per year.

Montreal Serai is a theatre of protest. It draws its modus operandi from the tradition of jatra and the dramaturgical approaches of Utpal Dutt, whose *Kallol* ignited Bose's boyhood imagination, and draws its content from the inequities in the world around us. The former's influence in Bose's plays, about which he has spoken in his interviews elsewhere, can be more ably analysed in India by Indian readers, who can also discern the imprint of such non-Indian masters as Dario Fo, Fugard and Augusto Boal. So, I shall confine myself to the Canadian component, the realities of which, no doubt, have their parallels in the Indian context.

The world around Rana Bose is Montreal; Montreal is a rich and vibrant city, old by Canadian standards, but it is also the seat of Parti Quebecois, the political party that jealously guards French-Canadian identity. This directly and adversely impinges on the rights of immigrants of non-French descent, even if they speak French fluently, as Rana Bose and his group do. Given the Parti's two targets of white anglophone Anglo-Saxon Protestants

(WASPs) and non-white immigrants, the latter is an easier one to shoot at. When the CBC (Canadian Broadcasting Corporation) aired a two-hour French documentary *To Disappear: The Destiny of the French Nation in Quebec?* Rana Bose was promptly in the news with his reaction:

> At the end of it all, the finger points at immigrants. The complaints used to be that immigrants are illiterate, lazy and are going to take our jobs away. Now they say these people are too literate, too educated, they work too hard and they're going to take our jobs away. (*Montreal Daily News*, 15 Feb. 1989)

This quotation exemplifies Serai's hard-hitting and tell-it-as-is approach to its own role in theatre, magazine publications and Canadian society. The inequities built into the Canadian system are clear to any thinking Canadian:

One, demographical statistics show that we are fast moving towards a time when those of British or French descent will be outnumbered by those who are not. Thus, the whole concept of 'two founding nations', which, moreover, exemplifies a basic injustice in its exclusion of the First Nations, needs to be revisited.

Two, the history of Canadian immigration during the last century shows different segments when there was a massive infusion from a given country; each group was tethered at the margins and made to work its way up. Thus, Icelanders, Ukrainians, Germans, Chinese, Japanese, have all been ostracized at different times for no reason other than their origins. South Asians have been at the whipping post (the world over?) for the last few decades.

Three, in the Quebec context, the prejudice against immigrants has resulted in numerous flareups, a recent one being Parizeau's charge that the secession referendum was lost because of non-French immigrants in Quebec.

Rana Bose tilts against different evils in the Canadian Establishment: for example, at the government's patronage system in *Baba Jacques*; at incipient Quebecois racism in *Nobody Gets Laid* and general racism in most of the plays. But his plays are not uni-dimensional; they span a range of issues and this becomes a very mixed blessing indeed, demanding an intellectual alertness and acumen that a Canadian audience is not used to giving to the margins.

Bose has thought deeply about the relationship between the centre and the margins, or the tribes and the borders as he calls them. In a talk I had with him, he said:

> Everything that is happening around us has made me wary of borders. Borders will always exist, but I believe in extending borders, extending and bringing them to the centre, of blending. Blending is for me a kind of political assertion that is inclusive. I feel that I can just as well define the terms of inclusion rather than demand to be included. We have to go beyond making demands to be included. We have to be taking the lead; saying, 'Want to join? Come on.' We should lay the ground rules for inclusion. That way we won't have to worry about being excluded.

He refers to all bureaucracy and government agendas as 'tribes' and, in *Five or Six Characters in Search of Toronto*, he punctures the balloons of all tribes such as self-righteous fundamentalists, egocentric art critics, brainless sports jocks, leaving them totally deflated. While the Establishment tribes are his main target, he does not spare the so-called 'victims'. Some of his most sparkling characterizations are reserved for Indians in Canada. He shows them to be opportunists who can conjure up every trick in the book of advancement strategies for charlatans.

Even though the white Canadian audience will make the topical connections, I feel that, as in the case of Salman Rushdie, the most appreciative audience might still be those in India, and Indians in Canada. In *On the Double*, for example, the mother is a priceless example of the Indian mother who does the shopping for the family—be it for high-funda tape recorders not yet available in India, or for an equally braggable bride for her son. In Bose's party scenes, we meet the successful and wannabee Indo-Canadians, flaunting their material wealth, and their hollow status signposts, such as being seen with ministers.

The dialogue is fast-paced, and the lighting and music add to the visual and aural complexity of a multiplicity of things coming at the audience at the same time. Most of his plays are complex, and there is always an Indian penumbra playing against the backdrop. It might be a tortuous brother-sister bond as in *Nobody Gets*

Laid, or a humorous mother-son relationship as in *Baba Jacques*, or an oppressive political regime as in *The Sulpician Escarpment*, or a topical reference as to the Babri Masjid episode in *Five or Six Characters*.

The Death of Abbie Hoffman [named after the well-known American radical activist] is one of the most complex of his plays. Nilambri Ghai, one of Serai's actors, told me how long it took them to workshop the play. Bose trains the troupe members with seminars on theory and practice, and they spend long hours mentally moving themselves into their space, their role. When I asked him to talk about that play he said:

> Abbie was a symbol of a time that is now lost forever, no matter what. It was a time of rebel spirit laced with enormous comic-relief about the contrite ways of the Establishment. The passing of Abbie, his 'death' to me was the defeat of ideology and the birth of the right-wing trash 'common sense' counter revolution. So the larger picture is the ignoble collapse of passionate belief in change—that is the death . . . The 'death' has to go from our lives. Abbie, I love him. He was a bend in the road. You know, I got the idea for Abbie from Badal Sircar's *Michhil* or *Juloos* and I kind of readapted it to the 90s. Abbie was a refreshing look at everything, a direct attack on hypocrisy, and his death was symbolic of a passing of an age of youthful challenge. So I trashed the right as well as the boringly correct. So it caused some confusion.

The spectator of a Bose play comes away reeling at the experience of total theatre, where lighting, music and stage effects collide and spin along with fast-paced dialogue; the reader can experience the words more clearly but misses 'the visual attack on the senses' in the words Bose uses for his memories of Utpal Dutt's theatre.

Uma Parameswaran
May 6, 1997

Theatre Notes on a Bright October Morning in Montreal

So, I am travelling on a suburban train from Kolikata to Bordhoman (pre-colonial names for Calcutta and Burdwan) and a thin, wiry man with a roach-like countenance (carefully cultivated to resemble Cantinflas) whips around and slaps a doleful-looking, height-beleaguered guy right behind him, smack on the face. The sound ricochets through the compartment, even though the sliding doors of the speeding train are sliding open and close, noisily. There is a momentary stillness in the compartment. But before anybody can intervene, the slapper tells the slappee, 'Disgusting, ugly-looking, nerve-wracking, monstrous, blood-sucking son of a bitch. . .' and the slappee looks totally shaken, confused, bewildered. His jaws are locked and he is going into rigor, even foaming. The slapper turns around and addresses the rest of the compartment, 'Mosquito. . . big, swamp monster. Just killed it and saved your life and lives of many others in this train. Now look here.' And he fishes out a brown ointment tube and starts going from passenger to passenger, hawking its merits in dealing with insect bites. 'Only one rupee.' There is mirth, enjoyment, carefully cultivated disdain, coming from different corners of the compartment, as well as encouraging looks. The slappee has bounced back from his near-death experience and has whipped out a bagful of the same snake-paste, which he is also trying to push with great enthusiasm, even though his cheek is getting increasingly rose red, almost. This performance is unforgettable.

It is 6 o'clock in the evening. 1969. Rush hour, on the corner of Russa Road and Hazra Road in Calcutta. A group of us bring out our drums and other noise-making equipment and with the first sounds, the crowd clears the broad pavement and we start a street play, recently developed in our college hostel. It has to be quick. The topic of the play is the hypocrisy of the ruling United Front government. A two-person band on the edge of the performance area strikes up an indigenous version of 'Mack the Knife', with Bengali lyrics. Somebody in the audience says, 'Brecht, Brecht's tune'. Another says, 'No, no! Kurt Weill. I am damn sure.' Three other members of the troupe, with shawls wrapped around them, stand guard at three different corners, watching out for plainclothes policemen who are known to attack such guerilla theatre shows with absolute ruthlessness. The play ends without incident. The audience love it. The troupe disappears into Calcutta's proverbial millions. Theatre on the run.

1974, St. Louis, Missouri. Charlie Mingus and his jazz troupe are performing at Washington University's Graham Chapel. I am manning the light mix-board. He is playing one of his famous pieces. 'Passive Resistance.' He has a Hitchcock-like profile. But he is cool, suave, to the extreme. The band slowly winds down. One by one, the pianist, the saxophonist, the drummer, all leave after playing solo bars each. Only Mingus is left. He is playing the lead tune, as well as the thumping tempo on his bass. On cue, the lights have shrunk to a single zone, tightly around him. There is a stunning stillness in the audience as Charlie's bass attack is synchronous with every heart in the audience. He has dedicated this performance to those who have opposed America's war in Indo-China for the past decade. Mingus' notes are like a heartbeat that must spread. Suddenly, I notice, he has started moving off the stage, while his fingers keep moving in the air. The bass remains on its stand, alone. He is headed out towards the wings and yet the sound persists in our chest! What a performance! The follow spot frames him to stage left and he is gone. The audience erupts into applause. One more act that is hard to follow. Forever registering in my memory banks.

1959, maybe 1960, maybe later, I am not sure. I am sitting with my father, watching Utpal Dutt's *Kallol*, in Calcutta. I am about ten years old. This play is about the mutiny of the Indian Naval ratings against British rule, in 1942. The bow of the ship INS Talwar has been erected suddenly out of nowhere on the stage. And believe it or not, trap doors pop up on stage, and in the audience, as if we are all on the deck. The ship's guns rotate and fire thunderous shells, while naval ratings storm down the stage. There is fire, explosions, tracer lights all on stage, craftily cued in by the master of all lighting designers, Tapas Sen. I am awed by the sheer performance, the spectacular epic element of the production.

1992. Montreal's Carbon-14 perform *Krieg*. Powerful choreography, techno-sound craft, combine with intense political angst about the times we live in. The small blackbox, Usine C, situated in the east end of Montreal, is a powder keg by the time the show is over. The audience dribbles out, whispering 'wow!', in French only, of course. The coldness of the Po-Mo [post-modern] era has set in. Our theatre group has also just finished a run of *Death of Abbie Hoffman*. This was an adaptation of Badal Sircar's *Michhil*, written and directed by me. There is surprising similarity between the Carbon-14 production and *Abbie*. But our play has only one fog machine as opposed to Carbon's 14(?!). We perform, in a small community theatre venue. Our sets are explosive and experimental and so is our sound. But our publicity spread is limited and the volume is low, so the audience is never very big. Ours is a beggar's opera and we love the poverty, or at least we have made a virtue out of it, nevertheless. It seems we isolate ourselves with our own angst. Besides, the city's leading drama critics do not find us adequately cuddlesome. In fact, we are nettlesome. Anglophones, or rather non-francophone theatre people in Montreal, are into 'safe' theatre. The condomized act. By themselves or when they are into patronizing minorities as a demonstration of their inclusiveness, in opposition to the French sector, which is supposedly less pluralistic. Also please do not rock the boat. Let us be the non-controversial segment of society that suffers with dignity.

Carbon-14, of course, have received literally millions in funding. Our theatre troupe, Montreal Serai, has of course never received any funds. Some people say we are the ethnic or minority version of Carbon in Montreal, without the spectacular effects. Which is very cute and consolatory, but tiresome, nevertheless, when one attempts to balance the books after each run. And I do not even want to expound, in these pages, on the issues of exclusion, marginality, borders, etc., which have become the forte of professional analysts of otherness, who continue to battle the cuts in arts funding and its consequent effects on 'minority' arts in trendy magazines, while being duly funded by the Canada Council. What really appeals to me, or, what I have really begun to settle down to, is an alternate sense of 'globalization.' Theatre is really an act of sublime seduction. A performance that must combine all possible, attractive means, drawn from all corners of the world, from all experiences, and blended into an entertaining mix that makes the viewer sufficiently disturbed, angry, agitated, energized and ready to react conclusively against the state of affairs in our world. The music, the choreography, the words, the poetry, the colours, the tones, the effects must all blend in a contemporary cauldron, which, by itself, must become a defining act of defiance and creativity. Political roots remain significant, but only if they do not become compulsive. As a theatre troupe, we must remain in the community, apprenticing newer and newer faces and developing new believers. We must do it with our own resources and without using the crutches so willingly extended by condescending patrons of the majority communities, who are constantly in search of ethnic novelties.

Love of performance is rooted in an intimately-held belief that epic and spectacular acts leave a deep mark on the human conscience. And conscience must always be cultivated, in an artistic, accessible manner. It requires blending. Blending is key. It is like performing on the borderlines of different cultures. Weaving in and out of different dance styles, music genres and performance methods. In effect, different sectors of the audience can find significant elements of their own life experiences on stage and yet comprehend a contemporary topicality. All this requires technology. Equipment. Technology must be there, always as an enabler, to enhance the effect on the conscience. And as this demand on blending different forms in a popular, attractive manner increases, there is a need for funds. Funds that are not available for experimentation. That is our reality.

One bright note, for today, though. As I finish writing these notes, the Nobel group has discovered Dario Fo finally. Talk about seizing some centres!

Rana Bose

On the Double

1986

3-Woman Chorus	Jennifer Chew Kiran Dholakia Amrita Choudhury
Story-Teller (with a yo-yo)	Himmat Shinhat
The Wimp Son	Kalpesh Oza
The Father (Also Writer)	Vasu Seshadri
The Mother	Kiran Dholakia
The Daughter	Amrita Choudhury

The inspiration for this play was provided by a theatre performance by a group of New Delhi women players. In form and content, however, this play reflects a Montreal and Canadian reality.

This play is not intended to be performed on a proscenium stage. It should be performed in a space carved out of the audience area, or the audience should be dispersed all over the theatre space. One cube or box is necessary for sitting down. The players are dressed in black clothes, with colourful sashes, head bands etc. In the version performed by Montreal Serai, *live music was provided by Serai players.*

Scene 1

Three women come in, with jerky movements—two freeze, the third mimes switching on a TV. With each flick of the channel she makes the sound 'click' with her mouth—the other two verbalize the channel changes and mime the rectangular screen with their hands framed around their faces. They switch accents and physical mannerisms. In another version of the play, the three women start the play by singing a parodied version of the old Beatles favourite 'If I fell in love with you, would you promise to be true?'

(CLICK) 1. J.R., if you still haven't found out what I have been up to, hey! Rest assured I'm stoking your goose in my oven, honey! Ewing stocks and all!

(CLICK) 2. (*puts on shades*). Hi! The name's Sonny Crockett—this muh buddy Rico—the word's out—you got 9/10ths of a second to clear out of this strip—or me and my buddy gonna make mince meat patty out of you and sell it to the sharks. Yeh! (*Mimes holding a handgun, while she takes an aggressive kneel-down stance.*)

(CLICK) 3. Why do I insist on Preparation H? I insist on Preparation H because I can go golfing, I can go swimming, and there is no pain. It's true, with Preparation H, there's no pain. Preparation H—with Biodine.

(CLICK) 1 (*sound of the Journal's theme tune and woman starts speaking with Barbara Frum accent and body movements*). We will now talk to Mr Larry Smith, a hog farmer in Mudhead Creek, Oregon.

(CLICK) 2. 'As far as I'm concerned, the Canadian government is too damn far to the left, with all those subsidies that it is giving to the Canadian hog farmer. We 'merican farmers think that's a bit of un-American activity going on out there—like the socialist stuff—next thing you know they's gonna stuff the *Das Kapital* down your throat.'

(CLICK) 3. As a woman, I like to feel secure—anywhere I go, anything I do and with ultra thin baby powder scented maxi pads—why, they even fit into my purse.

(CLICK) 1 (*male style*). I use speed stick by Mennen. Goes on smooth, goes on dry and stays dry. Wide enough for a man, heck, made for a man! Speed Stick. By Mennen.

Blackout.

Small musical riff. Blues boogie style. Can be done live by male in black, with guitar, wearing shades and a fedora style hat. When man finishes the three women come back.

WOMAN 1 (*rolling up sleeves, fake cigar in mouth*). Hi, I'm a single woman. I came to Montreal twenty years ago to do a Ph.D. in Biochemistry. It didn't work out. I drive a snow plough for the city and I love to hang out at singles bars—lots of heat and action there. Got to relax, you know. I put in a hard day—nine to five—sometimes the night shift. It's a dog-eat-dog world—but I can be soft—sometimes I put on milkbone underwear. (*Winks, spits and walks away. Turns around.*) And, by the way I hate tampons that have a baby powder perfume on them. (*Walks back.*)

WOMAN 2. Hi, I'm a mother—mother of three—I own the depanneur on the corner of Pine and St. Urbain. I am demanding, opinionated, contemporary, and I love that Rico—love the way he licks the Sealtest yogurt under a mean blue haze.

WOMAN 1 (*different accent*). Hullo, I am a wife and a social worker (*clears her throat*). I am presently studying the psychological ramifications of sociological alienation on the siblings of second generation South Asian teenage girls living in Brossard with their parents in semi-detached condominium cottages with two-car garages.

WOMAN 3 (*looks lost*). Hi, I am a sister, and I'm working the late shift at Dairy Queen. I had to struggle with my parents to take this job. My mum says—she is all for woman's liberation—that's why she is saving money to send me to university (*gap*) so I can find the right man. My father does not beat up my mother—that's not our style—he beats on the TV set instead—to stop the image from slipping up constantly. (*She mimics her father*).

WOMAN 1. Now a woman can mean different things in different places, right? Here we are thousands of miles away from the country of our birth, right? Thousands of miles away from Barodá, right? From Beliaghata, right? From Ghat Kopar, from Sangrur, right?

ALL THREE. Wrong!

WOMAN 1. We are only a few feet away. Because Baroda is just around the corner—you make a left on Mountain Sights, and there you are. Sangrur is right next to the Metropolitan—you take the l'Acadie exit—Ghat Kopar is on Taschereau Sud—keep going till the fork on the road—and Beliaghata is . . .

ALL THREE. Brossard!

All three women turn around and put colourful shawls around their shoulders. Two men appear from either side, like they are scrutinizing the women, head to foot. This section may be done in a hiphop style, intermittently.

WOMAN 1 (*subdued*). I am a woman.

WOMAN 2 (*subdued*). I am a mother.

WOMAN 3 (*subdued*). I am a wife.

WOMAN 1 (*subdued*). I am a sister.

MAN 1. Yo sis, talk to me, talk to me.

MAN 2. But a broad is a broad, yaar.

MAN. What it is, what it is!

ALL WOMEN. Yes, we are all broads.

MAN 1. You broads have been told several times over.

MAN 2. Not to hoop and not to holler.

MAN 1. Not to cackle like a bunch of geese.

MAN 2. And not to check us out, like we were sex objects or something.

MAN 1. And besides, your body is weak . . .

MAN 2. Your world is bleak . . .

MAN 1. Your pace is timid . . .

MAN 2. Your life is insipid . . .

WOMAN 3. . . . So smother your desires.

WOMAN 2. . . . And jail your minds.

WOMAN 1. . . . And shatter all your hopes.

ALL THREE. In lonely days and lonely nights.

Change of style to more positive.

WOMAN 1. But we do know a few things.

WOMAN 2. And we do know a good fight.

WOMAN 3. And as such we present our play.

ALL THREE. On the double, tonight!

Blackout

Scene 2

All characters turn their backs to the audience. Man 1 comes to the front of the stage. He is in the process of getting ready to go to work. Woman 2 is busy, pretending to comb a child's hair.

HUSBAND (*nervous wreck. Looks for tie, then realizes it is around his neck. Mimes looking for socks in drawers—throws everything out*). Kamla, Kamla, where the hell are you?

KAMLA. Where the hell do you think I am—would you like to try getting Munni ready for school?

HUSBAND. I cannot find my socks, dammit.

KAMLA. Have you looked in your shoes, dammit.

HUSBAND. Shit, there's a button missing from my shirt . . .

BOTH TOGETHER. Shit! Why didn't I/you fix it last night?

HUSBAND. May I give my humble yet important opinion? Was I to dream at night that I'd have a button missing in the morning?

KAMLA. All right, don't shout so much. I'll fix it after I've done Munni's hair.

HUSBAND. What else do you think I do but get up early? But I can never find anything where I left it. Now I can't find my handkerchief.

KAMLA. It was lying on the floor. I washed it. Take another one from the closet.

HUSBAND (*in utter frustration*). Oh gee, how many times have I told you not to touch my things . . . but of course you love to be the typical Indian woman . . . always picking up everything behind me . . .

KAMLA. Oh yes, of course—now it's my fault that I've washed your dirty handkerchief. On reaching the office, you would have told your male cohorts, 'Such a drag she is, nosing into everything.'

HUSBAND. Forget it. I don't want to listen to your nonsense first thing in the morning. Where is my cornflakes? (*Walks to the back of the stage.*)

KAMLA. Where is his cornflakes? Where are his dirty socks? Where is his dirty handkerchief? How many times have you washed my socks? I mean it's OK with me that your problems are my problems, but why can't my problems be your problems too . . . instead of yours being ours and mine being only mine.

Freeze and blackout.

Scene 3

Woman 1 and Man 1 have returned from work. He sits down and turns on the TV. Woman 1 is reading a letter. Man watches TV and mimes taking off his socks, tie, sweater and throwing them in all different directions.

KAMLA. There is a notice from the school.

HUSBAND. Hummm!

KAMLA. There is a parent-teacher meeting.

HUSBAND. Hummm!

KAMLA. Try to come back early on Thursday.

HUSBAND. Are you going to do something about supper, or are you just going to order me around? (*Turns off TV and walks away. There is a knock on the door. Kamla rushes around and gets the place in order.*) Kamla, Kamla, where the hell are you? Somebody's at the door . . . Here, put these keys on the dresser.

Kamla opens the door. Woman 2 and Man 2 enter. Man 2 has his shoulder up in a funny posture.

HUSBAND. Hi, Vicky, how's it going?

KAMLA. I will go into the kitchen to make tea.

WOMAN 2. And I will follow you into the kitchen, naturally.

HUSBAND. I'm glad you dropped by, 'cos I tell you, I was getting dead bored here all by myself.

KAMLA. All by yourself? Wasn't I here with you?

MAN 2. Heh, heh, your wife, she has a sharp tongue!

HUSBAND. Yeah, sometimes. She is usually very quiet. Now watch this. Kamla, Kamla!

KAMLA. Yes, I'll be with you in a minute!

HUSBAND. See, I told you. Kamla, bring some tea!

MAN 2. Just tea? (*like a jerk*).

KAMLA (*entering*). Well! Start with these, I'll have supper ready soon.

MAN 2. You make delicious pakoras! Hah, hah!

The women bring a tray with tea and snacks. Both men turn their backs and start talking in gibberish, very serious, prolonged gibberish. Occasionally you hear 'Reagan', 'Mulroney', 'Challenger', 'Marcos',

'Canadian dollar', 'Rajiv Gandhi', 'Computers', 'New blood'. Gradually the two women come to the front. The men recede to the back.

WOMAN (*to Woman 2*). You know, when they talk politics, if you listen carefully, they basically always agree with each other.

WOMAN 2. But they always find something obscure to rave and rant about . . .

Both women now put on papier mache masks that have striking resemblance to the two men. Woman 3 passes by with a placard. Placard has a drawing of a naked bum with water dripping on it from a lota *(a brass pitcher used in India, with water, in lieu of toilet paper). Sign says 'Ancient Indian device to cleanse the soul'.*

WOMAN 1. Without the *lota* . . . we would never have made it to where we are now . . . which civilization has the *lota* . . . which? . . . none. Because when we don't use water, we become unclean and when you have an unclean body, you have an unclean mind . . .

WOMAN 2. Bullshit . . . *Lota* means we remain backward . . . to the field, early in the morning, in the middle of winter . . . it's an absurd, indecent practice . . . it is outdated . . . The mass use of toilet paper is the only answer.

WOMAN 1. What about pollution? Have you ever thought of that aspect . . . we cannot afford toilets . . . so you will have the whole landscape littered with toilet paper . . . who will pick it up, ragpickers? Never! . . . You need a new caste for that . . . and none exist. So what will you do? And besides, toilet paper is not even reusable.

WOMAN 2. *Arey*, shut up . . . technology has always solved these problems . . . technology is the answer . . . With the new Prime Minister we will be stepping into the twenty-first century before it is here.

WOMAN 1. Your twenty-first century is a disaster and a debacle for the great Indian spiritual and philosophical tradition.

WOMAN 2. Toilet paper, my dear, is a sleeping giant. India must wake up to this sleeping giant and history will unfold itself . . . full of new dreams, new lifestyles, new successes . . .

WOMAN 1. Without the *lota*-all will be lost. The glorious tradition of our forefathers, of our spices, of our mythology . . . Even a sadhu going to the Himalayas always carries no worldly belongings except a walking stick and a *lota*.

WOMAN 2. Oh, come on! In fact . . . in fact . . . without our penchant for the appropriate use of technology maybe we can find a happy medium to combine the latest with the future . . . and discard the ancient . . . With the proliferation of computers all over the land . . . maybe we can produce a specially textured printout that will also find use as toilet paper . . . as an end use!

The two scream at each other—Lota/*Toilet paper—alternatively and then suddenly stop abruptly.*

WOMAN 1. But politics is politics.

WOMAN 2. Yes, politics is politics. . . and whisky is whisky.

They mime drinking whisky and make the sound glug glug glug. End with these words. Freeze. Man with guitar plays another quick riff.

Scene 4

WOMAN 2. The dude's back from work, dog tired . . . mumbling about office intrigue . . . now who cares?

WOMAN 1. She comes back from work, dead beat, keeping her sorrows to herself.

WOMAN 2. He flops down on the love seat: 'Sweetheart, can I have a bourbon?'

WOMAN 3. His friends come, they discuss politics, and real estate. She makes the food.

WOMAN 1. He stomps out with his friends, she stays home to listen to the whine of the vacuum cleaner on the rug.

WOMAN 2. He returns home late, she stays up for him.

WOMAN 3. He drinks and pukes all over, she cleans up after him.

WOMAN 1. He has a deep sleep, she wakes up with a cold sweat.

WOMAN 2. And she wakes up before he does in the morning and makes tea for him.

WOMAN 1. He runs helter skelter, looking for his socks.

WOMAN 3. She finds them in his shoes.

WOMAN 2. And this is the way the wheel keeps on rotating:

WOMAN 1. One two, one two . . . (*like in a ship's galley. Two other women arch their hands in opposite directions and pull the oars.*)

WOMAN 2. The wheel of day.

WOMAN 3. The wheel of night.

WOMAN 2. The wheel of morning.

WOMAN 3. The wheel of evening.

WOMAN 2. The wheel of Karma.

WOMAN 3. The wheel of Dharma.

WOMAN 2. The wheel of tradition.

woman 3. The wheel of life. One, two, one two, one two. . .

Fadeout

Scene 5

Man with shades and fedora playing with a yo-yo, up stage left.

WOMAN 1. Ram's brother is a writer, he flirts with the mind, with the written word—he is a progressive.

WOMAN 2. He lends his voice to the mute . . . outside the house that is!

WOMAN 1. . . . It is past 10 o'clock, my daughter has not returned home as yet (*worried*).

MAN 1 (*always to the audience, in a nervous manner*). Maybe she has an important rendezvous set up with a possible employer.

WOMAN 1 (*pacing*). She should have returned by now, it is getting very late.

MAN 1. Maybe she got held up on the 'Metropolitan'.

WOMAN 1. But she is very young, and she is a girl, also her brother and father should come in any moment now. (*Man 2 walks in, city slicker, shirt buttons open etc.*)

MAN 2. Ma, I don't see Bani, where is she?

WOMAN 1. I don't know . . . normally she is here by now.

MAN 2. You are very indulgent with her. Some day she will get herself into trouble.

MAN 1. He means she will be pregnant by a white man.

WOMAN 3 (*entering*). Will you quit worrying on my account for God's sake. I won't be the cause of any disgrace to the family.

MAN 2. Where have you been so late at night?

MAN 1 (*nervously for her*). Nowhere, nowhere, just here and there.

WOMAN 3. Who are you to ask me? Do you ever tell me where you go?

MAN 3. Exactly, does he ever tell her where he goes?

MAN 2. You see that, Ma, you see that, see the way her tongue flies.

MAN 1. He means she talks like a Canadian girl.

WOMAN. Don't say anything to her. I will do the asking myself.

WOMAN 3. I went to see Jack's father. He said I could do some graphic design for his consultancy on a freelance basis.

WOMAN 1. You left at ten in the morning and you are returning now after eight. Don't you realize what you are saying?

WOMAN 2. I wanted to come back earlier, but I missed the six o'clock bus.

MAN 2. What a lame excuse, you missed the bus, shit! When you knew you would miss the bus, why did you leave the house in the first place? Working for Jack's father! Bullshit! All you needed was a pretext to leave the house and loaf around

Crescent and Bishop . . . I'm fed up with all these lies . . . anyway, Ma! I'll be late for dinner, don't wait up for me. I'm going to Vijay's. He's got the new Madonna video. (*Wicked eyes. He leaves.*)

WOMAN 2. Bunch of yuppy jocks . . . sit around and swig Budweisers and hum and haw.

MAN 1. . . . And wait for Madonna's nipples to pop out, but they never do.

WOMAN 1. It is different with him, Bani. You are a young girl. You should come back home before dark.

MAN 1. Women are hopeless in the dark (*eyes twittering*).

WOMAN 2. Ma! I only went to see somebody for a job . . . I want to come up with some of the money for school . . . don't you see that?

WOMAN 1. Yes, but back home it was easier . . . anyway, I have something to tell you . . .

WOMAN 2 (*starts backing out. Man 1 says 'Oh! Oh!'*). Not another proposition from a tall, handsome, fair-complexioned, Kayastha business executive, is it Mum?. . . and who, it just happens, does not have an immigrant visa.

MAN 1. Or a tall, handsome Jat Sikh from Jullundur, with several video stores. Hmm, hmm, but the Sikhs are in the dog house these days.

WOMAN 1. Do not pretend to be ignorant, Bani. These people have been approached by your brother. One of the brothers went to Doon School with Rajivji.

WOMAN 2. But I want to complete my Masters.

WOMAN 1. Masters! You've got to be kidding! What for . . . These people are not going to wait.

WOMAN 2. So why don't you find another young virgin bride for them?

WOMAN 1. What's that? You know damn well that your father and brother have been negotiating this match for you. How can you dare say that we break this arrangement? Your brother feels the same way—if it's not going to help you any further, what is the point in going through a Masters, and once you do your Masters, you will want to do a Ph.D.

MAN 1. And once she does her Ph.D. . . . it is too late . . . she's out of the marriage market . . . Indian men only study upto MBA.

Mother leaves in a huff.

WOMAN 2. Yes. I know my brother feels the same way as well! Professionally, he is a writer of progressive fiction. He writes of love and turmoil and revolution in unknown republics. He writes of the revolt of the working class intermingled with the sweet aroma of romance in a faraway Middle East sheikhdom. At home he is just a brother—an upholder of decadent male patriarchy.

MAN 1. He is just protecting the little sister.

Blackout.

Scene 6

WOMAN 1. My husband is a writer . . . What are you writing, husband?

MAN 2 (*sitting on a cube, pretending to write*). A story, wife.

WOMAN 1. What kind of a story is it, husband? (*Looking at the audience.*)

MAN 2. The story of a young woman during the days of the British Raj in India, wife.

MAN 3 (*with yo-yo*). Ah yes! The Raj is hot (*counts on his fingers*), *Passage to India, Heat and Dust, Jewel in the Crown, Gandhi,* Edwina and Nehru (*bites his tongue*).

WOMAN 1. What is the theme of the story, husband?

MAN 2. The woman goes to her husband's home with great desire and expectations in her heart. But her dream never comes true. He has taken a vow of perpetual celibacy. She quietly accepts everything that comes her way.

WOMAN 1. Why does her dream not come true?

MAN 2. Because her husband cannot understand her feelings.

MAN 3. He has very little of his own. There is numbness in his vitals.

WOMAN 1. Does her husband try to understand her feelings?

MAN 2. Why are you pestering me with all your dumb questions?

WOMAN 1. Tell me, does her husband try to understand her feelings?

MAN 2. You will not understand all this. You are a woman and this is literature.

MAN 3. Exactly, here is a fish, and there is a bicycle.

WOMAN 1. Why? Is not literature a reflection of life, of reality?

MAN 2. Look, quit hassling me, will you? Literature is simply . . . (*lost in creative looks*) literature . . . an experiment with the unknown.

MAN 3. Bullshit that sells!

WOMAN 1. Alright, I understand. Here, drink your milk, I am leaving.

MAN 2. Shit! Now she's gonna be mad again . . . Don't get upset please . . . I promise you that we will make that trip to Europe this summer.

WOMAN 1. This is to say as though the destination of our emotions is a trip to Europe . . . And my husband has written a story about a woman's emotions. Here I am a woman, serving milk to my husband and revving my engines on the runway to an emotional high . . . (*She stops with glazed eyes . . . breaks into a smile and rushes over to her husband.*)

Hey! What do you say, why don't we go out and do something crazy tonight? Maybe rattle the old cage a little, you know. Shake down your tree a little. What do you say, eh, eh, eh? (*She wraps herself around him. He gets nervous, drinks milk and splits.*)

MAN 3. This was another scene from the play. But the subject is not covered as yet. As usual, we are hammering home the issues. As usual, we are being political. After all, anything that is not silly as shit is political. Anything that is not sheer mindless entertainment is political. Anything that takes sides is political. Anything that is not sold at Perrette's is political.

Freeze, blackout.

Scene 7

The three women appear again. When one speaks, the other two mime the scene.

WOMAN 2. Hi, I'm the sister. It's that time of my life when the rest of the family starts giving me those looks which mean 'this house is not going to be yours for much longer now . . .' I must look 'prospective'. Even the women giggle and poke me with their fingers. . . 'Guddi, it is time you got hitched!'

WOMAN 1 (*chewing gum*). She was born in Canada, she grew up in Canada, she went to CEGEP in Quebec. Her father is Vice-president of URANUS 2000—a Canadian holding company. Her father attends receptions at the Ritz with Yvon Lamarre, Pierre Des Marais, gives $20 tips to the doorman. He wears Giorgio Armani. Her mother wears a Banarasi brocade sari—There she is in the 'Living' section of *The Gazette* giving mean shitty looks to the wife of the Pakistani ambassador. Her father travels all over the world.

WOMAN 2. Her mother worries—God only knows what he does during his jaunts. But he must be hot 'cos he's got the bucks coming.

WOMAN 1. Now the girl is in Concordia. She hangs out on the fourth floor—that's where all the kids hang out, make the connections, flirt a little, where the lockers are. She's got a guy she's been seeing for a while—they're pretty close—but so what! Her mother says she's got someone big set up for her.

WOMAN 2. Someone from Faridabad. He's got a cement factory, a bicycle factory, and an export brand dal-moth factory. And he chews paan. (*All three of them pretend to chew paan and scratch their groins, in a typically male fashion.*) He visits here often. Last time he was here there was a heated discussion in the living room on the exact percentage of extra-marital sex amongst Indians living in Montreal. Now who really did a survey of this? Anyway, the point is that she's gotta go through this ritual. Her parents are gonna tie her to a chair in the living room and she will be discussed, examined, measured, and then she will do Kathak.

WOMAN 1. Yes, all Indian girls growing up in Montreal must learn Kathak or Bharat Natyam. And they must do Kathak in front of their 'prospective' in-laws. Her father, who is the V.P. of URANUS 2000, a Canadian holding company, who attends receptions at the Ritz, and who pays $20 tips to the doorman, who travels all over the world, who wears Giorgio Armani suits will screw up his eyes and say, 'Tradition must be maintained.' *All three say it together.*

Scene 8

Woman 1 sits down on the cube, chin in palm, disgusted looks. Man 1 comes in and announces 'Prospective in-laws'. Man 1 goes out, brings in son. He holds a placard which says 'I am the man from Faridabad who owns cement, bicycle and dal-moth factories.' Son has back problems. Slumped, unsmart posture. He comes in, clears his throat to attract attention. Daughter visibly disturbed by appearance.

WOMAN 2 (*to audience*). I am her future mother-in-law. I have come to look at my future daughter-in-law.

MAN 1. She seems good-looking.

MOTHER. You always like everything at first sight. Rush, rush, rush—always rushing around. In New York, you rushed around and bought a JVC cassette deck without even looking around. It has only one deck. Everybody in Faridabad is now buying Sony cassettes with two decks. Now everybody will say we came to New York and could not find a two-cassette deck. All these *chamars* and low castes going to Kuwait are also coming home with two-cassette decks. Always rush, rush, rush. And you, son of an engineer . . .

FATHER. Will you shut up and look at her closely. I think she is a shade darker than they told us. What do you think, Ricky?

MOTHER. What can he think?—Stand up straight—He will do exactly whatever I tell him to do. It is my kitchen she will inherit, not his. Ha!

SON. Every time you give your opinion, the girl decides she needs more time to think over it. This is our third trip to Canada . . .

MOTHER. You keep quiet. Nobody has asked you for your opinion. Don't open your mouth without permission. I haven't even seen her figure. You do aerobics, my dear? All the girls are doing aerobics in Faridabad these days.

WOMAN 1. I do work out once in a while.

MOTHER. Work out? What work out? What does she mean by work out? (*All go into consultation. After a while, she goes back to the daughter*).

MOTHER. I haven't checked her height as yet —

SON. She looks tall enough for me . . .

MOTHER. You shut up. Nobody asked you for your opinion.

FATHER. How can you tell when she is sitting?

SON. By now I am experienced. I always see them sitting. I always see you two arguing, I am always told to shut up. I always like them, I am always ready to marry, but you must always weigh them, you must always measure, you always argue and then you negotiate, and it always breaks down and on to the next one who is always sitting and I must always shut up until I get your permission and I never get your permission. (*He starts bawling.*)

WOMAN 1. And the hollowness of the whole thing . . .

MOTHER. Oh my God! She speaks!

The whole family cowers, while the young woman rises to stage front.

WOMAN 1. . . . is that right here now in the midst of a quiet hilltop residence overlooking downtown Montreal, or in Flushing in New York for that matter, I will be examined, scrutinized, dehumanized and chastised because my parents believe in the upkeep of tradition, while his parents believe in obtaining a thoroughly modern, English-speaking, 'phoren' import to install in the already large acquisition list his family has. And for all this the poor boy and the poor girl must wait for the gentle nod from the parents that signifies permission. Permission is religion—permission is the last straw that our parents have. That's why they have given it religious sanctity.

The in-laws rush out. They say they will go to Florida where there are more 'prospective in-laws'.

MAN 1 (*stops playing with his yo-yo*). When an Englishman has an emotion, his first instinct is to repress it. When an American has an emotion, his first instinct is to express it. When a Canadian has an emotion, his first instinct is to ask for a government subsidy, and earn the wrath of the American. And when an Indian has an emotion, he must look for permission.

Lights slowly fade out.

The Death of Abbie Hoffman

(An adaptation of Badal Sircar's *Michhil*)

1991

Chorus	Amrita Choudhury
	Lisa Foster
	Angela Smith
	Anirban Choudhury
	Prasun Lala
	Patrica Ward
Old Person (Nina)	Nilambri Ghai
Young Person (also Nina)	Anita Choudhury
Mr Hydroxy Cue	Himmat Shinhat
Director	Rana Bose
Set Design	Aziz Sharafi
Lighting Design	Andy Calamatas
Music (Arranged, Composed and Performed)	Himmat Shinhat
Costume Design	Lisa Foster
Make-up	Angela Seth
Song Lyrics	Rana Bose
Singers	Himmat Shinhat
	Raja Lala
	Babla Choudhury
	Lisa Foster
Back-up Singers' Choreography	Amrita Choudhury
Solo Dancer	Angela Seth

Scene 1

Audience walks into a foggy, cool room. Seating arrangements are in a maze-like formation. Blue tracer-like follow spot directs audience to seats all over the auditorium. Orchestral music, with a low note bias. The control has started.
In the dark background, a big mural hangs, made from masks of faces. Different sizes create a 3-d effect at the back. At the beginning, the lighting creates a grim quality. At the end of the play, these same masks, again with lighting, will seem to look pleasanter. Audience legs hang down from rectangular risers and cubes, placed like a maze.

When play begins, chorus of six come in with leader in front. All are dressed in grey ragged clothes—dark lines on faces. Leader walks in like she is muttering religious incantations. Actually she is saying 'unanimous' and the rest of the chorus is saying 'consensus'. Occasionally each one will have doubts and will say, 'But sir, may I . . . I also think . . . On the other hand . . . I can't see a thing . . . Can I . . . But why not? . . . Actually . . . Do I have to . . . Second time around the maze, they move in jerks and stop- -hands freeze in dance-like movements (with music). Leader's eyes are very stern. Eventually, the leader is more powerful—her voice of 'unanimity' rises above all, and she moves through them with very threatening looks.

Suddenly there is a massive explosion sound and powder flash is seen at one end of the auditorium. All lights go out and a tremendous scream is heard from within the chorus—as if someone has been assaulted. In the dark the chorus moves through the alley, purposely bumping into the audience—asking them questions directly.

In the dark (soundtrack of Japanese bells), they all look up to the sky.

1. Who turned off the light? Hey! Who turned off the fucking lights?

2. Someone blew the fuse, man. Overloaded the lines.

3. Bullshit! It's a fucking solar storm again! I tell ya! It's a new galaxy in the works.

4 (*very crude theatrical laugh*). New galaxy! My ass!

5. Watch it! Where the fuck do you think you're going?

6. Ooh! You touching my boobs!

4. I did not! I heard a scream.

10. Somebody's been murdered!

Solemn silence for a while.

2,4,6. What, c'est pas vrai—murder is impossible.

5 (*lights a match*). Depends on what is murdered, darlings (*all light matches and huddle*).

6. What is murdered? (*Repeat in several tones. At this point all except 1 confer in gibberish for a while, in a huddle, and then looking at each other and continuing in a huddle they say,*. 'Gamma, alpha . . . delta, beta'. *Then they break off and spread out.*)

2. On January 3 1889, Nietzsche collapsed into insanity.

3. On June 21 1984, Michel Foucault was pronounced dead.

4. In the same institution where he researched madness.

2. He thought on the fringe . . .

6. He had a Eurocentric ego.

1. I have no ego. I have four pairs of socks, I wear my shoes loose, I never call in sick and I use nasal spray.

2. I can't think any more.

1. She is from Kennebunkport.

3. Somebody's been murdered.

4 (*nervous*). Somebody's been stabbed and her body's been whisked away.

5. Nonsense! Nobody's been murdered.

4. Then somebody's fallen into a hole.

1. Yes! A manhole—a man-made hole.

2. It's a paradigm shift.

3. It's a pendulum swing.

4 (*to No. 1*). Do you have thoughts!

5. They have dug up all the streets.

6. Why do they molest all the streets every year?

4 (*to No. 1*). Do you have thoughts?

1. I am not a cat. Only cats think.

2. Well, do you see in the dark?

5. Last year, they dug up the Champlain Bridge.

6. Every year it is Champlain Bridge.

5. This year it is Champlain plus the Turcot interchange.

6. Last year, it was Champlain plus Metropolitan.

5. The year before, it was Champlain plus Decarie.

6. I think Champlain was a world leader. He was one of us!

5. Yeah! Champlain was bigger than Descartes, Kant and Nietzsche. He was the father of Hegel.

6. Yeah! He was the brother of Freud. Carl Jung was his neighbour. His mind worked like a flash!

1. Does anybody have a flashlight?

2. Does nobody carry a flashlight?

5. There must be smokers amongst you. Do you have a match, sir, you, sir? Ma'am? (*Asks the audience.*)

He lights a match. Lights come on simultaneously. Police sirens sound. Masked Man (Mr Hydrox Cue) rises up from within the audience. Militaristic looks. Shaft of light on him alone, while police light turns. Across the room, a follow spot takes a big 'Q', sound of water, floods. All players climb onto audience area. Blue watery lights in maze.

MAN (*walks in the maze, slowly*). (*Bilingual.*) What's going on here, eh? What's all the racket about, eh?

1. The lights went out, sir!

2.There was a scream.

3. Someone's been killed by a solar storm.

4. Someone's been stabbed and her body whisked away!

5. Yeah, into a manhole, sir.

6. Was she wearing any clothes?

MAN. Shut up! There's been no murder. There's nobody. How dare you talk about murder.

Chorus mumbles amongst itself, huddled.

1. But sir, we . . .

2. Saw with our own eyes.

3. There was a scream.

4. Must have been stabbed and the body whisked away.

MAN. Shut up! (*Walks about.*) There's nobody. There's no murder. Don't start rumours. Don't malign.

A woman from within the audience, or from another end, comes running in and collapses onto the floor.

1. There see, I told you it's her . . . she was murdered.

4. She was stabbed and whisked away.

MAN. Shut up I said! Go home! Stop spreading rumours. Nobody's dead. (*Bilingual.*)

2. What a mess . . .

MAN. Yo! I said get back inside your homes.

3. There she is . . .

4 (*in French*). I told you there was a murder.

5. Wait a minute. Is she murdered or is she dying?

2. Oh my God. What a mess!

5 (*in French*). It is a slow process.

4. Somebody whisked her away . . .

They whip around and look at No. 4 and then slowly approach the body.

5. If she is not dead, how could she have been murdered . . . To be murdered, you must have been alive. Listen to me.

4. Sir, you're thinking the unthought. She was stabbed and whisked away . . . that's it. That's just her body.

5. Ah! Just like that?

4. Just like that!

5. Why was she murdered?

3. Who said she was alive?

4. I heard her scream.

2. Those who scream, they are the ones who . . . in here. (*Points finger to his head, winks.*)

MAN. I said shut up! Hiss! (*All cower a bit.*)

2. There's the body.

MAN. Silence! (*He walks about angrily.*) Listen, if you want to discuss, go somewhere else . . . For us, there is nothing to discuss. C'est claire? It is over, OK?

ALL CHORUS. It's over, OK! Unanimous consensus.

3. But sir . . .

4. We saw the body.

MAN. I said the word is 'Nobody is dead' . . . There is nothing to discuss. And go home before I chase you all out. Hiss.

The chorus scurry away like rats in the dark. Young person rises up slowly . . . The man does not notice her.

YP (*smiles*). I am the one who was killed. You know me, don't you? I was killed today. Now, just a little while ago . . . (*Goes close to each member of the audience*) It's me who's been killed . . . just now. Yes? I was killed right now. Every day, every fucking day, I am killed. I was killed yesterday. I was killed the day before. I've been slowly poisoned for the last ten years and I'll be killed this week, next month I will be killed.

Man is totally oblivious. He walks around.

For the last several years, they have been finishing me off and you come and you don't see me. What do you watch? Why can't you see me? What do you come to watch, anyway? Look! Look at me! Here, I am the one . . . every day, every week every year! You know! They've found a new way to kill me, and there is agreement all around. Isn't it amazing, they all agree, everybody agrees nowadays. There are no disagreements. Old enemies have become friends. Old walls have collapsed. Everybody fucking agrees! It's like the whole world is fighting to agree! And I had always thought history was progress by conflict. Instead there is only . . . there is only . . .

The Chorus from the wings say 'Consensus'. She builds up to a peak and then slowly collapses and rolls over like a corpse. Music of wind sounds. The other man steps over the body and walks away. His shoe-steps resound in the auditorium. The Chorus come back in a line, humming 'Bolo hari, Hari bol, *Dump the body in the hole.' They lift the body up, high above their shoulders, turn around to the music. Some of them start chanting . . . Slow fadeout.*

Scene 2

As sound of the Chorus slowly fades away, older person (Nina), with almost insane looks, comes rushing into the maze. S/he hands out cards to the audience. Cards say different things. (Consensus, sacred truth etc.) OP will, in the beginning, ask everybody to be silent (shush!). Even to the soundtrack (towards the ceiling). She will distribute these cards strategically. She wears a funny hat.

OP. Don't tell them! I gave you these cards . . . Don't even tell them I am here . . . I am a journey person, I travel, I watch, I am a bystander, an onlooker. I watch processions, funerals, parades, manifestations, demonstrations, pickets, walkouts, lockouts, strikeouts . . . I hear hymns, chants, screams, prayers, pleas, psalms, slokas, screams! Screams! Lots of screams! (*She starts walking around the maze.*) Here, let me see . . . (*On her knees, very loud*) *Allah ho Akbar, Sat Sri Akal, Garb Se Kaho Hindusthan Hamara!* (*Very soft*) Halleluiah!

Halleluiah, Halleluiah! May God be with you. *Le Seigneur soit avec vous, et avec votre esprit,* amen!

She opens her eyes and asks members of the audience, if they have not already done so, to come and sit in the middle sections of the maze.

Come along, come along, take these seats (*she takes them by the hand*). We shall see a *'juloos'* or a *'michhil'* which means procession, manifestation (*in French*). *Juloos* means a long journey in Persian—an endless journey. I have seen many *julooses*—for food, for clothes, for salvation, for revolution, processions of refugees, processions for guns, butter and flood relief, processions of St. Jean Baptiste, Carifete, Mardigras, O Canada—processions with ministers and kings in waiting and trade union leaders, arms locked, processions for peace, . . . processions with stars, processions of taxi drivers, Iranians and Haitians mainly . . .

As she is going around in the maze, talking to members of the audience, the Chorus comes back, in a quiet semi-circle, and huddles near the riser. At the end of her above piece, OP is swept aside and her hat gets knocked out by the Chorus. There is background music. All Chorus wear tight white masks or hold them in front of their faces.

CHORUS (*very violent*).

Consensus, Consensus,
Hezbollah, hezbollah.
BJP, Babri Masjid,
New World Order, Now or Never,
Jarry Falwell, The job is done,
Hochelaga, Chateauguay
Maradona, Now or Never
Janet Torge, Jean Dore
Cite Libre, Celine Dion
Ayatollah Khalkhali (*Eyes*)
Gabriella Sabatini (*Fluid tennis strokes*)
MC Hammer, DJ Cool
Ne touche pas, Hydro Q (*hiphop style*)
Serbs, Croats, Tamils
Campeau Belanger, Spicer
Dan Quayle, Joe Clark

Who do we want: Ben & Jerry (*twice*)

(*Chorus leaves. Soft music—instrumental theme tune.*)

OP (*picks up her hat slowly. Holds it in her hand*). When I was a little girl, one day early in the morning, somewhere between fall and winter—it was a sweet morning—there was a chill in the air—the sunshine felt wet and moist—I walked along a road, holding my father's hands. Dry leaves cracked under my feet, wild flowers swayed in the wind. I held my father's hand and followed the road. The road meandered along and disappeared under my feet. Old roads came and went. New roads appeared suddenly. (*She walks through the maze.*) At times, all roads seemed to vanish. Beyond a point, you could not see. It seemed the road had come to an end. Then suddenly, there was a bend, and beyond the bend a new road appeared like a flash. Just when you thought all roads had come to an end, a new one would appear. Roads! They appear and disappear and leave you wondering. Once we would come to a bend, my father would say, '*Ma cherie*, let's go back.' I would say, 'Just a little more, till the next bend.' (*She walks a little faster.*) I could see a new road further beyond. My father would say, 'Let's go back—that's the end of the road . . .' And this would go on. . . I would say, 'Let's go on . . . just a little bit further . . .' and he would say. . .

(*Voice of Chorus*)

CHORUS. Let's go back, *ma cherie*, it's the end of the road!
Let's go back, *ma cherie*, it's the end of the road!

OP. Just a little further, there's a bend ahead. (*She repeats and moves out fast.*)

CHORUS (*frenzied shouts*). Hey! Come back! It's the end of the road. Nina, Nino, Nini! *Ma petite cherie, reviens!*

Hysterical Chorus comes running in and scatter throughout the maze and confront the audience.

1. Hey, you, have you seen a young girl? (*She holds a small mirror to the audience.*)

2. You, have you seen her?

3. She's got big eyes, and a snub nose?

4. Long legs, she shaves her pits.

5. She's naive and stupid.

6. She's short and thin.

1. She's little in years, little in wisdom, little in knowledge.

2. She's crazy, she loves to argue all the time.

3. She's sexy, she's always making a point.

4. She's stupid, she doesn't understand.

5. Have any of you seen her?

1 to 6. Have none of you seen her?

They stop in a freeze and then spread out in the maze.

1. Lost. One girl. Her name is Nina. She has a snub nose and big eyes. Anybody with any information please contact the *Gazette, La Presse, The Daily, The Link, Journal de Montreal, Le Devoir,* and Pierre Foglia, he knows.

2. There has been an assassination or an abduction. A young girl named Nina has been assassinated or abducted. Anybody with any information please contact your nearest police station or the SQ or the GRC or the CSIS or the force Canadienne . . . We must have her body.

3. Hello, Lacolle, Phillipsburg (*Like she is using a cellular*), Niagra, Jean-Talon, Park Avenue, Guy Favreau . . .

4,5,6. Guy Favreau?

3. Canadian Immigration. Hello . . . Hello. Large eyes, snub nose, long legs, shaved pits.

4. This the CBC Radio Canada. Broadcasting at 100, 000 KW with our transmitter on top of Mount Royal, we can be heard simultaneously in Baie-Comeau, Sherbrooke, Temiscaming, (*cut*) Abitibi, lower North Shore, Kampuchea, (*cut*) Kampala, Nairobi, New Delhi, (*cut*) Mascouche and Repentigny. Can you hear us? (*To the audience, repeats. Others help the audience to say 'yes'*).

AUDIENCE. YES.

4. A girl named Nina is lost. She has been stabbed and her body whisked away into a manhole. Anybody with any information on any part of her body, mind or any other attribute, please call Dave Bronsttetter, Louise Penny, Augusta Lopez, John Kalina.

3. No! Not John Kalina, he is away for three weeks always!

5. Hi, this is radio station CJUT where hip is never and crack is dull or dull is crack. You have a problem? Hey, check us out.

Can tennis give you AIDS?
Do elbows have jaws?
Do bicycles ride fish?
Hey! Is politics getting to you?

This is 'Notions and Motions'—a community program designed and altered by RADIO ALTERNATIFE, the alternate network for alternate people—We alternate news and views with motions and notions—and right now we are looking for Nina. Yes NINA—N-i-n-a. Anybody out there with any information on Nina, please call 999-CJUT that ain't no party-line, honey. If you are calling long distance, well keep it that way honey, we do not reverse charges. Hey! Now! We are looking for Nina. N-I-N-A. Long, tall, thin and stupid. Last seen on the corner of Hutchison and let me see . . . Trafalgar Square.

6. Nina, come back from wherever you are. You have no choice in this matter. There will be no negotiations—there were never any treaties. In fact, your demands are stupid, absurd and bizarre. Everybody here agrees. We are happy the way we are, we have no problems, no conflicts, why do you want to disturb the peace? You have no choice, you have to come back.

1 (*sobs*). Your father and mother have been crying all day and night. They go to bed crying in each other's arms. (*Next person*)

2. Your brother and sister cry as they play, they play and they cry.

3. Your uncles and aunts, your cousins and in-laws, they eat and they cry, they cry as they eat.

4. Nina, come back, we promise to clean all the manholes and sewers.

5. You'll get whatever you want.

6. No, she won't!

5. Yes, she will. She will get whatever she wants. She will get her own cellular, CD, and cop buster in her own Lexus.

1. She'll get her own detached cottage and a satellite in the sky.

2. She'll have happiness, peace and . . .

6. She will have religion!

ALL. Yeeeeup! She will have Religion, 'cos Religion is back. (*Quick song*)

CHORUS. The pope is from Poland, o yeah
Albanians want more pizza,
East Germans wear jackboots,
The wall is down in Berlin town,
The KGB takes NDG
The pope is from Poland.

2. Gorbachev wants investments, no technology, no MBAs . . .

1. Yeltsin says, 'Over my *matrushka's* dead body'—He is a tricky motherfucker—he ends the Cold War to get money from the West—why I worked so hard? President Bush says . . .

1 (*Bush's voice*). We are on the threshold of a new world.

2. I have drawn a line in the sand . . .

3. There shall be peace, happiness and salvation for all.

4. The United Nations is in the United States—which is in lower Manhattan! (*Eyebrows*)

Group from the Chorus do hiphop-style song 'Woh, Nina!' The lyrics are contextual and change, reflecting current headlines or topical issues.

Scene 3

OP has walked in after end of rap song.

OP. Her parents named her Nina or Nino? Doesn't matter. Thousands of parents with thousands of Ninas. Nina means small, young. Nina means enquiring . . . It means green, raw, immature but questioning. Nina is not a closed book. It is an open mind. Lots of questions. Lots of arguments. Lots of debate. Lots of conflict. Ha, ha! Lots of conflict . . . Nina means there is no final answer, no closed chapters . . . (*Deep breath*) Nina is alive when the debate is on. Nina is lost when truth is sanctified, because, because, I tell you, no truth in this world is sacred. Nothing is sacred. (*Laughs*) Nothing is forever.

CHORUS (*in echo style*). Nina . . . a . . . a!

OP (*becomes humorous in her walk and gestures, almost teasing*). She is lo-oo-st (*mimics echo*).

CHORUS. Nina, you better come back.

OP. Heh, Heh, she ain't coming back to this dumpy old house!

CHORUS. Nina, you got no choice.

OP. Sure she does, she'll come back to a new house, a new home, a real home, not this old dump, for God's sake what do you think she is?

OP (*back to normal tone, smiles*). You remember I told you about the road? But these days the road goes round and round and you come back to the same road. You look for a bend and it ain't there, it's the same road again, eh! Have you ever thought of that? What's missing? Do you know? You don't want to . . . You don't want a bend in the road?

A loud scream is heard. Horrible scream of 'Nina'.

What's that? Who was that? God! Did you hear that scream? Like someone—you know? Was it at that bend? There? Beyond that bend? I must find her!

She runs through the bend and leaves. The Chorus comes running in. All members of the Chorus wear local papers like Le Devoir, Globe *and* Mail *etc. like dunce caps on their heads.*

1. Check out the papers! Check out the papers!

2. Saddam arms himself again.

3. Britain and France supply rockets.

4. US supplies bottled gas.

5. 'We shall not allow this evil to happen on this earth again,' warns President Schwarzkopf.

4. Prime Minister Barbara McDougall says: 'It seems he has not learnt a lesson.'

6. Martina . . . will not go back to Czechoslovakia even though things are changing there. The President is a playwright, you know . . .

1. Hmm? Wonder if Brian was a playwright . . . then maybe.

2. Pele signs contract to run for PQ in Jonqueire: 'We must get the negro vote'.

3. Otherwise the Mohawks will pow-wow downtown, next time esti . . .

4. Le Roi Jacques wants out.
The King of Quebec wants a bigger paycheck
like the Queen Mother at least.
(*or he will disappear into a manhole*).

5. Trudeau teams up with old flame Lise Payette to make a film of disappearing gold fish in Kenny Wong's China Pavilion in Brossard.

6. Mick Jagger will play lead fish, yeah!

1. Westmount declares sovereignty . . .

2. Speed limit will now be five mph . . .

3. Quebec police not racist, says Quebec priest.

4. Canadian space center will now be located in the Ville Marie Tunnel.

5. New research in the space center will explore ways of remov-

ing leaks in the tunnel. 62,000 jobs will be created.

6. New Big O roof contract will go to SOS—Salif Omar Salim, Kuwait's biggest tentmaker. 62,000 jobs will be created.

1. Kuwait and Quebec will merge as one country. Oil and Hydro will drive both economies. 62,000 jobs will be created.

2. British mag Private Parts claims Mila has taken to the bottle also.

CHORUS. 62,000 jobs . . .

3. 50 ton slab falls from sky on Civic Party Headquarters. Nick was not hurt. He was in between parties.

4. Guy Bouthillier and Robert Libman form new party: Mouvement Quebecois pour moving sidewalks.

5 (*faking Indian guru's voice*). Spiritualism alone can save this fucking world. Join me and the rest of my fucking gang for a special, fun-filled, yoga-dipped cruise in the fucking Caribbean.

Sound of Montreal subway comes suddenly. Whole Chorus pretend to be holding on to hand grips in the subway and lurching forward. Take off hats, bodies lurch to a stop.

1. Yo! Bottled water (*like a hawker*) from Cajun country—Here's your last chance to buy clean pure water in this continent. All the way from Baton Rouge, Louisiana—Bayou Blues . . . the only brand that carries the authentic aroma of spiced jumbalaya when you pop the cork. Now or never, now or never, *maintenant ou jamais* . . . $17.99—bargain basement—here take a whiff (*to audience*), uhhh! Smells good, you ma'am, hear it, can you hear it, can you hear it—buckwheat zydeco . . . *ils sont partis*—listen closer, listen closer, authentic french flavour Bayou blues *doucement*, attention, buy two you get a third one free . . . quench your thirst. Yes, I . . .

2 (*to No. 3*). What did you say?

3. Nothing.

2. I heard you say something! What you looking at?

3. Nothing.

2. Oh yeah! I saw you looking at my shirt.

3. So?

2. So you were looking at my shirt, eh?

3. So?

2. You look at shirts all the time.
You dirty old shirt-looker
You drink white wine, right?

3. Yes, occasionally.

2. I knew it, I knew it!

3. Knew what?

2. You dirty old shirt-looking, white wine-drinking faggot—I know you—bet you work alone in a shoestore.

3. So . . .?

2. See, I know you—now why would anybody work alone in a shoestore unless he has a dirty mind?

3. What you talking about now?

2. Listen, you guys, I hate you and them fucking short-haired feminist shits.

3. Hey, watch it man—it ain't gonna be so easy, you know—you guys think you are on a one-way street. No other view allowed (*all lurch to one side*).

4. One-dimensional world. (*Each turn their heads to each other.*)

5. Linear progression.

2. PC—political correctness.

6. No conflicts now.

1. We don't know.
We can't tell.

3. There was no discussion.
There was nothing to discuss.

4. Everyone agrees.

1. No debate.

3. No conflict.

4. No discourse.

ALL. Everyone agrees! Boom.

1. Attention! Attention (*like the metro driver at the stations Berri-de-Montigny, UQAM etc.*).

4. You're stepping on my toes.

5. Can't help it—it's too crowded.

4. You could have waited for the next train tabernac!

5. Then somebody would have said, 'Why didn't you take the earlier one.'

4. Then you'd have a problem.

5. Right! Whether to take the earlier one or the later one.

4. You're right.

5. You're right, too.

4. We're both right.

3. Why don't you move forward?

2. Yeah, there's lots of space up front.

6. Yeah, the seats are empty.

5. So what! I will not move forward.

4. Me too! I refuse to move forward.

1. What's the problem man, the train is moving Why we gotta move, eh? Don't make sense to me.

2. Yeah, right! (*All the bodies are crowded together in a heap.*)

6. But there are lots of empty spaces, there.

1. Just don't worry about it, man—it's somebody else's problem.

6. You touching me.

3. It's the train—it's making me do it—it's not me.

4. You mean the train is touching her.

2. I guess there's nothing you can do about it.

5. Yup! Nothing you can do, the train is in charge. Nothing anybody can do . . .

1. 'End of the line. Last station. Please get off carefully.' (*All try to jump off together.*)

2. Heh! My shoes—they're left in the train.

3. Come back next time.

They all run off. Train sound fades out. Lights fade out.

Scene 4

After subway sound fades out from previous scene, OP's face is seen behind the mural. She has virtually merged with the masks. Looks kind of insane. Almost crazy smile. Eyes dart. She slowly comes out. First smiling, then laughing louder and louder.

OP. I scared the shit out of you, didn't I? I think people should do whatever the fuck they want to do. What do you say? I am against all that pig shit like big corporations, big government, big acid spouting chimneys and big cops with big nervous fingers when they see big black kids in big little burgundy, playing big basketball—I mean you know all that . . . but this is all the hip shit that everybody likes to dump on . . . it's OK with me . . . but you know what else I hate? I hate big road signs, I hate big direction signals, I hate cul de sacs, I hate 'no turning', I hate 'bridge freezes before road', . . . and I'm really pissed off when I see 'Yield', or 'Prepare to merge'. But I know, it's their signs, their roads, their triumphs, their order, their fucking agenda . . . I gotto wait it out, every few decades, the dust settles—the clouds move out, the roads reappear . . . I gotto go . . . (*repeats and leaves*).

As she leaves, lights fade and guitar music begins. Lights fade in. Only two from Chorus come in. Man and woman. They are two totally different people. She has a red jacket, headphones and reads a book. He has a green jacket, fedora hat and smokes a cigar. The flavour of this scene is in contrast to the rest of the play. The two display far more emotions and sensitivity in their acting style. The music track plays a guitar lick from Jimi Hendrix, like 'Foxy Lady' etc. To disrupt her music, he purposely puts his foot on the riser and the music shuts off magically. Twice. He tries to establish an irritating superiority over her.

1. You looked rather grave yesterday. (*Clearing his throat.*)

2 (*slowly turns her face*). Oh! I thought it was you who looked grave! (*Silence.*)

1. 'Grave' is actually not very . . . correct terminology, you know.

2. Well, gee, you were the one who used it first! No?

1. Well! I guess . . . I was . . . I guess . . . (*silence for a while*).

2. Why is it incorrect anyway? I mean . . . hey, don't you guys (*to audience*) wanna know?

1. Well, because it suggests a relationship with death and dying . . .

2. Ah! Relationship with the dying?

1. No, that's not what I meant. What I meant was, it insults the dead! It is deathist . . .

2. Oh! Deathist! For a while I thought you were hinting at some kind of . . . sleeping with . . . necrophilia or some such thing.

They both stare out over the audience for a while. A droning robotic sound starts building up and then stops.No. 1 puts his hand onNo. 2's breast simultaneously. No. 2 has no reaction. No. 1 looks to see and then drops his hand in resignation. She is then startled.

2. Why did you do that?

1. Do what?

2. Take your hand off?

1 (*clears his throat and gets up*). Well, uh-h, along with freedom of speech comes certain restrictions . . . Unrestricted activity can be perilous . . .

2 (*goes after him in a 'put on' seductive fashion*). Oh, I see! Perilous?

Did you say? Hmmm. But without knowledge, there can be no democracy, and there is no knowledge without action, my dear—and action is often the ability to think of the 'other'. Were you thinking of the other?

1. Uh! Just a minute. (*Takes his hat off.*) What is this 'other'? Everybody seems to be talking about it these days? The 'other', the other, well, what is this other?

2. The 'other' is the unthought, my dear. Unexplored territory. The unknown frontier. The other side. (*She runs her hand over his face, without touching him. His eyes closed. A dancer comes leaping through the maze with a long trail of coloured cloth in her hand. His eyes are closed and he is controlling himself.*) It is uncanny, gruesome ideas, crazy, modern, zany and unfettered—that is why there is no morality to thought. (*She pretends to kiss him.*) As soon as thought functions, it liberates or enslaves. (*Dancer throws several pieces of cloth into the air. They come down slowly.*) Thought itself is action—my dear, it moves whatever it touches. It is guerilla theatre. (*Dancer has left. No. 2 is virtually on top of him. He opens his eyes.*) Do you understand? It moves whatever it touches. (*She kisses him gently.*)

1 (*hurriedly gets up*). Did I move you when I touched your breasts? Did I? Tell me? Well, did I? Did I move anything? Tell me? (*She walks away from him. Her eyes closed in anger. He approaches her, then walks back.*)

2 (*to audience*). Did you move anything? Did you ever move anything in your entire life? Did you? There is this other fucking problem—that has—that has made us all clinical and glib actors in every stage. Feelings and emotions are objects of suspicion and ridicule. The sudden impulse, the subversive act, the voice of pain, the cathartic overflow, the three o'clock roadblock has been undermined by an overdose of systematized dissent—and you, my friend, you are at the core of this passionless act (*points to No. 1*).

Chorus with four people come in slowly and assume frozen position on riser or in front of mural.

1. Controlling emotions is a sign of maturity and necessary compromise. This is the era of correct terminology . . .

2. You don't understand, you don't understand at all . . . I am . . . talking about another time . . . long ago.

CHORUS. Long long ago. (*Leap into a tableaux as if from nowhere, orange glow behind them, and with percussion acapella style*) Marlon Brando, Lenny Bruce, C Jam Blues, Velvet Underground, Miles Davis—cool jazz man.

1. Well, I know Charlie Sheen, REM, Midnight Oil, Kevin Costner, Rocket Eshmail, Eddie Murphy, Ninja man, Vanilla Ice, Bill Murray, and Spike Lee.

2. Right! Right! Yeah! Right! and Spike fucking Lee . . . Arnold the exterminator has been put in charge of the new order . . . Emotion is strictly forbidden.

CHORUS. Acting is strictly forbidden! (*Same style as before or change to one at a time—very physical, emotional—dancer accompanies*). Lee Strasberg, the name is Dean—James Dean, Rod Steiger, Stanislavsky, Theeee Method, Geraldine Page, Group Theatre, *Streetcar Named Desire, Hud, On the Waterfront, East of Eden, Bonnie & Clyde, The Graduate, MASH,* and *Waiting for Lefty.*

They collapse in a heap. Blackout and explosion sound—followed by the sound of water running out of a bathtub. Lights on 1 & 2 again.

2. You thought you moved me? You thought you touched me?

1. Within allowable and discrete limits.

2. You are boring, you know. You are fucking boring. You cannot touch anything, man. You're busy screwing around with norms and ethics, rules and regulations.

1. Ask me what is my methodology . . . and I will tell you . . . tell me to write a grant, ask me—

2.—about employment equity and you know! Huh! You are like a party . . . party . . . apparitchik.

1. That's okay, it's in Word Perfect 5.1 Spellcheck.

2. There's too many of you everywhere. That's it! You've seeped into every institution—in college newspapers, women's groups, union meetings, art councils, environmental lob-

bies—everywhere except native groups.

1. That's a coming.

2 (*she comes close to him aggressively*). Hey! You don't understand! I said you are taking everyone for a ride.

1. That's a mighty serious accusation you are making there!

2. I couldn't get more serious with you. You do not know the difference between the sublime and the ridiculous, (*1 tries to interrupt several times*), between catharsis and repose, between knowledge and action—you're confusing all issues and getting everybody to groove on nothing (*laughs*), nothing. And then you think 'grave' is politically incorrect because it demeans the dead—don't you? Well! How ridiculous! How insane! How fucking insane, Mr Politically Correct! Look at him, Mr P.C.

1. Uh! Just a minute!

2. Just a minute, my ass—you've started the process of simplifying the debate—you're part of the problem—you've made a career out of the grey middle ground using soft terminology. That's why when you chew you sound like a liberal, when you walk you walk on the right—and you can chew and walk—Jesus! We have a problem right there. We're back to square one. No wonder everything is under attack.

1. I am standing still! You are getting spazzed out writhing in nostalgia and besides, let me tell you something. (*He puts his hat and cigar back on.*) Did you know, George Bush developed a thyroid condition just before the war. I mean, you know what I mean!

CHORUS (*in different questioning poses appear in a tableaux and they say things like*). You mean? Is that right? Could it be? Actually . . . Now, why didn't I think of that before! Hm, come to think of it. I wonder. Well, you know. Did you say it was the thyroid gland? Did the Pentagon know?

At the end, this scene blends into a song performed live 'My Glands'; a parody of the wellknown pop song 'My Girl.'

Scene 5

OP comes trudging along. She's got a lantern or a flashlight. She goes into a quick jog to one end of the audience. She is busy rummaging through a sack she carries. She finally finds a bottle, takes it out and has a swig. She is happy.

OP. I keep telling her—don't worry, you'll find your way home. She doesn't believe me. She thinks it's the end of the road. Now look at me, I kept losing my way and I kept finding a new bend in the road. My father would hold my hand tight. He would say let's go back. Uh-uh! When I grew up, mind you, I would lose my way too. But by that time my father was gone. What would I do? Ha! I would do something very clichéd. I'd take out my bottle and swig it down in big gulps and when I'd licked the last drops off—the sun would bob in the horizon—or at least that's all I remember. I have some friends who would say—'Look at her—she don't wanna face it.' But I'd always see the sun bobbin' in the horizon. And they'd see nothing.

The young person has come in from the other side—she's got a flashlight. She keeps her distance—hiding from OP.

OP. Now, let me see. Where is she—that one? Can any one see her! I have to see her. There is a road that I know . . . it's just a little after the first bend there, it's a narrow road with trees all over it . . . it's like a tunnel, but you can see something at the end . . . eh, you know what I mean? . . . Once I was with my father . . . and we were tired. The night was falling. There were only crickets . . . that was all we heard. If you looked up it was all dark. If you looked around there was nothing . . . just the sound of the crickets . . . that was all you heard . . . but then if you listened carefully . . . there! Can you hear it . . . can you hear it? A distant sound . . . yes! . . . So we followed that sound.

YP (*screaming*). I don't want to hear that story again. I've heard it many times before.

OP. Ah! She is here . . . Come here . . . I wanna talk to you. (*They are at opposite ends of the maze. YP tries to keep her distance.*)

YP. I don't wanna go on that road.

OP. It's not the old road. There's a new road.

YP. All roads are same here, I know that.

OP. No, this is a different road.

YP. I'm telling you, I don't wanna go to that old house on that old road.

OP. But this will be a new house.

YP. No, it's not true! There is no new house. It's the same thing with you every day . . . the same old shit routine dragged out in the streets and there are no breaks for me . . . and no explanations, everyday there is a procession, a rally. For what? For nothing! And I'm being stomped upon by your procession, your dreams, your ideas which don't mean a thing—in fact it's your procession that's killing me . . . I'm dying because there's nothing in your procession . . . don't you realize?

OP. Don't say that to me. It's not my procession. I did not call the rally. It's them . . . they called the rally.

The Authoritarian Man appears in a very militaristic posture. He walks through the maze clicking his heels.

MAN. Attention! (*All lights come up. OP and YP go close to each other inadvertently. They go and sit in the audience and quietly disappear after a while.*) Nobody's dead. Start the rally!

Chorus appears as a band with kazoos and whistles. They hum 'Tequila' and then at the appropriate moment, instead of 'tequila', they say 'No Problem'. By this time the military man has changed his garb in front of the audience. He has put on a pair of shorts and a tie. The Chorus jog around the maze and slowly prostrate themselves in front of him like they were doing push-ups. He now assumes a TV/spiritual leader role. Every time he makes a statement . . . the Chorus says 'Amen!' 'Hallelejuh!' 'Wah-wah!' in different languages.

MAN. Today I will talk to you about something very important.

CHORUS. Shhhh.

MAN. About the environment and the government.

CHORUS. Ahhhhh.

MAN. We are all born as babies, not as men.

CHORUS. Ah! Yes, come to think of it.

MAN. The Lord said, 'Children must grow up and become men.'

CHORUS. Hallelulah.

MAN. And you can't be a man till you have made a deal with your environment.

CHORUS. Amen.

MAN. To be at peace with your environment you have to make a hash of the past and the present and dish up the future. That is the task of the government, my children. (*Heh, heh, heh.*)

The future of the nation depends on grown men in government (*heh, heh, heh*). Grown men must tie together in a single bond. Our past, our heritage, our history, our land, our waters, our tradition and keep it alive for future business (*heh, heh, heh*).

CHORUS. Wah, wah, *tawba, tawba.*

MAN. Grown men must conquer all fears about conquering nature, because nature is for us to conquer. We all love the environment. Don't we? We all love the water. Don't we? The fresh air, the water, the breeze. There is power in the environment.

CHORUS. *Mon dieu,* this is very important, come to think of it. There is power in the environment.

MAN. Power through power. That is my message for today.

CHORUS. Power through power.

MAN. Power through power
Want not, waste not
Save power, have power
Sell power, have power
Have power, save the nation
Power through power

CHORUS. Power through power.

They line either side of a walkway, while the man slowly walks away, acknowledging them and ringing a little bell from his hips. A grim sombre music is heard.

1. God save our great nation.

2. And our great leader.

3. Without him all would be mud.

4. Everything is mud anyway, whisked away into the sewer by the flood.

5. All power to our nation.

6. All power to our people.

7. State power is what we want.

3. Power lunch is what I want.

CHORUS (*in unison*). What!

3. I want lunch. Power lunch is what I want.

He takes out a bag of chips and starts chewing on them.

All Chorus surround him like a pack of wolves.

2. What did you want?

3. Lunch. I want lunch.

He cleans his ears.

3. Don't shout in my ears.

2. She wants lunch. She wants to lunch.

1. Death to the terrorist.

3. I am ready to die for lunch.

4. Throw her in the manhole.

5. How dare you want lunch when I don't want lunch?

6. I think I want lunch, too.

3 & 6. We both want lunch.

They separate slowly into two camps.

1, 2, 4 & 5. What!

3 & 6. We agree, we want lunch, we want lunch. (*Repeat.*)

1. Death to the terrorists.

1, 2, 4 & 5. Death to the terrorists.

2. Long live the motherland!

4. Long live free speech.

5. *Allah ho Akbar.*

1. *Bande mataram.*

2. Beat up the bastards, throw them out of this country.

4. Fucking refugees! (*They start pushing and shoving each other.*)

1. To the plans of Abraham!

3. We believe in Gandhi, we want lunch.

6. Don't touch me, I warn you, don't touch me.

1. Bomb them to the stone age.

2. Send in the fucking Stealths.

3. Long live David Suzuki.

6. Long live Farley Mowat.

4. Death to cross border shopping.

3. Death to GST, estee.

1. Beat up the bastards.

They clash, punches fly, choreographed with lights, music, tai-chi movement. They all end up on the ground. Then they rise slowly as if in a tired walk. One of them, it seems, is carrying a human head that resembles the young person. Music.

2. Can you tell us please, sir, where is the *dernier recours*?

3. My son wants to join the KKK.

4. My factory has moved to Buffalo.

5. My daughter hates science.

6. Our lady appeared in Ste Anne de Bellevue (*makes the sign of the cross*).

1. New York needs electricity.

2. Via Rail has stopped coming to our town.

3. The 144 will have fewer runs.

1. Banning Kashtin was just an error.

4. I saw my aunt Nellie at the NDG food bank. She pretended she didn't see me.

5. The government will not pay for any more shelters.

2. We will have a new Forum. The city says it needs a new one.

3. The schools are full of Orientals.

They slowly trudge away, repeating what they have already said, except No. 2. She stays. No. 2 keeps repeating about 'derniers recours'. Scene fades into Scene 6.

Scene 6

2. Can anybody tell me where is the *dernier recours*?

She walks around in a slow fashion. There is a music score that builds up slowly. It has a searing quality. Under three separate spots at three levels we see No. 2, Man and Woman from Scene 4 in an embrace kneeling and YP and OP. In the beginning No. 2 continues about 'dernier recours', *YP wraps herself up with her hands and sits down as if in pain, shuts her ear off. Then she explodes.*

YP. Stop, stop it godammit, stop it! I know where it is, I know where it is!

OP. Oh! You mean you want to go home? Is that right?

YP (*after looking at her for a while*). No! You don't understand. I've always wanted a home.

OP. That's new. I always thought . . .

YP. It's not like, I don't have any roots.

OP. Oh! You mean you're thinking about what my father said?

YP (*looks at her*). I don't really care for what all the fathers have said. (*Walks away.*)

OP. Where are you going?

YP. Somewhere you've never been. It's through those fields. There are no roads this time.

OP. I don't understand anymore! You don't wanna go home, but you're off somewhere and there is no road! This is strange! (*She fumbles and looks for something.*)

YP. Yes! I don't wanna go home anymore. I wanna find a new bend and one that no one's been on before—one that you don't know, one that they don't know, it's not on any map—it's just a bend out there . . . only I will know. So, this time they won't see me. They won't kill me anymore. I will come like a wind, formless . . . I will sweep through and they won't know what hit them, I will climb onto them and they won't see me, I will grab their little throats and they will gasp . . . I will throttle their little glands till their desert smiles evaporate and they will stand there like apes naked . . . I will tell everyone there is no consensus—they can agree, but we do not concur . . . I will tell everyone . . . (*She runs off repeating her lines.*)

OP. I better go . . . I need my . . . (*takes a swig from her bottle and runs after YP*).

Music changes. Only spot on man and woman. They turn their faces. They have greased back hair, slick looks. After a sensuous embrace they stop, straighten their dresses.

WOMAN. Well, now tell me, do your thoughts menstruate? Do you think the unthinkable till warm corpuscles of blood trickle out of your head?

Long gaps in-between.

MAN. Do you still listen to The Doors and have fat joints on Arabian beaches?

They both mime like they are rowing oars in a boat. Fog starts to collect around them like they are in a boat in a fog. Music right through.

WOMAN. Does your blood sear a path through the grass for you to follow? A path that you thought did not exist yesterday?

MAN. Do you still dabble in Fanon and reinvent a past that does not exist?

WOMAN. Do you ever want to undermine all your sacred cows?

MAN. Is there nothing in this world that you and me can agree upon as being rational and correct?

WOMAN. Does Europe always hold the keys to correctness and order?

MAN (*looking far away*). Good question! Did the Roman Empire begin to falter after the triumphant declaration of a new order?

WOMAN (*puts her oar down*). Who, what are the forces in charge of naming things and what do the named feel?

MAN (*to the audience*). Are feelings like colonies that want to remain colonized?

WOMAN. The art of representation is getting to be pretty tricky. Scholars, newsmen and leaders have formed an alliance to colonize all others. If you ain't with 'them', you're with the 'others'. There is no debate. There is no common ground for peace in the valley. Lions and lambs can never represent each other.

MAN. Representation has become irrelevant. Images on the tube have captured the intellect. Anything done by the mob finds a political sponsor.

As she says this the rest of the Chorus appears, holding candles in multi-candle stands. They pass them by with hmmmmmm sounds, through the fog. Possible Gregorian chant. They are wearing black robes, heads covered, arms are bare. Man and woman join them and move away.

Scene 7

As the Chorus leaves to the chant, OP is seen on the riser. She is fiddling around with her sack. She is drinking, but she also sounds insane. YP slowly rises up while listening to OP. OP cannot see YP in the beginning.

OP. I just can't find her. She ran away. I told you all along—and you wouldn't believe me. Right? You thought I was dreaming! Huh! Actually I knew it all along. My father was right! It's the end of the road! There ain't no bends—it is a straight road. Everything is in order—who wants bends anyway? Fuck bends! Things are fine without any complications—I mean why look for solutions, when there are no problems. And anyway, you see this bottle! It's almost finished. I'm gonna take a few more swigs and head back—back all the way. I know the road back. You know it's easy downhill—Me and my bottle, that's all it takes—You'll see now.

YP. Just a minute!

OP. Who? Who was that?

YP. It's me.

OP. Who's me?

YP. You were the one who started off about the bend!

OP. What bend! What're you talking about?

YP. About the bend, for Christ's sake! In the road!

(Gap)

OP. You're dreaming! But that's okay! Here! Wanna have some of this? Nectar, pure moon! Makes you blast through the sky! Ever been high, kid? Like I mean really high? Here, take a swig . . .

YP. You told me about the bend!

OP. Gee, what's with her? Listen to me, kid!

YP. You kept telling me about the sun bobbin' on the horizon!

OP. Ah! You're talking haze now, sister. Haze! (*OP takes another swig. YP thinks for a while.*)

YP. What about your father?

OP (*jumps*). What about him?

YP. You kept telling me about him—and the bend in the road . . .

OP. Keep him outa this! You're tripping on something, or what?

YP. You said that he'd wanna turn back and you'd say just a little further and you don't wanna come back to this dumpy old house and he'd say let's go back . . .

OP. You're upsetting me, you know!

YP. . . . and what happened to the narrow road with the trees all over it. (*OP gets more unsettled. Starts staring out.*) . . . Like a tunnel and you could see something at the end—and then you'd talk about how you once told your father to go take a hike, 'cos he . . . (*OP gets up*) 'cos he didn't wanna hear you—

OP. . . . play Janis Joplin in the toilet.

YP. . . . right, but you loved to hear her scream 'TRY—Just a little bit harder'. Well?

OP. Just a minute, now!

YP. What's got to you, now?

OP. You're going too fast!

YP. And remember, the good laugh we had when you told me about the kid last year who wanted to know if Woodstock was a farm, owned by Bob Dylan . . .

OP (*laughs*). Fucking Bob Dylan . . .

YP. Remember, what you told him?

OP. Yeah! I told him Dylan was a dog who thought he inherited the Nation.

YP. Yeah!

OP. And a farm dog, 'cos he pissed always on the same old posts. No city dog would do that!

YP. 'Cos city dogs piss on each post they pass.

OP. Even when they run out of piss.

YP. Yeah and you said the trick was to be urban, and move along! 'Cos otherwise you'd be dumping all your life on the same posts—and then some day, some smart ass who owns the farm, is gonna get rid of the posts—or move them somewhere else . . .

OP. And then you wouldn't know what to do—'cos you'd be looking for that same old post to piss on and you wouldn't find it—so you'd stand around, with your bladder full—meanwhile they'd straighten out the place and make it look totally different—totally unfamiliar.

YP. Yeah! But nothing's changed really in the farm.

OP. You just can't see the posts. You can't see the wire. But you know, they got it all rigged up—if you cross the lines—zap! They've won, Nina, this time, Nina. They've taken over the farm.

The sound of the theme tune starts filtering in slowly. First it is grim, like in the beginning. Then it gets into a beat and a livelier rhythm.

YP. No, they haven't—they've got the whole farm spiffed up, looking good, that's all—like everything's settled, but when you get closer—the shit still smells the same.

OP. Listen, can you hear something?

YP. And every few decades, it's the same! The smart asses who own the farms, figure out new ways of spreading the shit! And the new pigs, think—ah, the boss is different, not like in my dad's time. The shit is not bad! Hell, it even smells good! And the bosses declare triumphantly—they've won!

OP. Hold it, hold it, I can hear it!

YP. And we scurry around buying into it. We've lost our shtick! We've lost our sense of humour, sister. We can't joke about the banality of the powerful, we can't piss on their sacred cows, we even worship in their temples, and the shit is still the same.

OP. Hold it, you're not listening carefully—

YP. Listen to what?—Stop playing games! (*The sound gets louder.*)

OP. That's it! It's them! They are coming

YP. Who? Who's coming?

OP. It's them. (*There is pride and emotion in her voice.*) The fools. They've finally got it together—this time. There! Can you hear it! It's them! Can you hear . . . Where's my . . .

(She puts on her hat, takes a quick swig. Chorus appears, dancing and singing. OP and YP eventually join them.

Scene 8 (Alternate End)

As OP and YP rush out into the wings, looking for the sounds from the Chorus, the music gets louder and the lights fade and one by one, different members of the Chorus appear in different parts of the theatre space. The music is a rock feedback guitar style. No. 3 weaves a dance pattern through the maze to the music.

When she finishes, the rest of the Chorus comes strolling through.

6. Yes, yes . . . we will go through those fields, where nobody's been before. We'll take a road, which is not on any map—we'll find a bend, where there was none before . . .

4. Because, this time they won't see us, they won't know where we came from, they won't know what hit them . . . and they will not kill us any more . . .

2. No! They can't kill us any more. We will come like the wind, formless—we will sweep through their valleys in the night, we will turn around bends and double back on them and they won't know where we came from.

5. We will not go by their order of things, we will not buy their definitions, we will not be caught in useless debates on their side of the street, we will trash their road signs . . .

6. We will tell everyone . . . yes . . . we will tell everyone . . . my friends (*holds the hands of somebody in the audience*), there is no

consensus . . . they can agree, but we do not concur . . . we will tell everyone . . . there will be no deals . . .

OP (*appears on riser*). We will climb onto them and they won't see us. We will grab their little throats and they will gasp. We will throttle their little glands, till their desert smiles evaporate, and they will stand there like apes naked.

All of Chorus start moving slowly towards stage rear. Lights slowly fade out on OP. Music crests.

The Sulpician Escarpment

1995

Jack Simard
The Brother
Sax Player
The Mother
Young Girl

Ace Chatterjee
Calcutta Drunk/Gangster
Anita
Mrs Chatterjee / Extra in line
Gene Burris
Jane Westman / Immigration Officer
Calcutta Drunk/Gangster
Paul DeCosta
Professor Amit Bose
Mordechai Sassoon

Georges Beriault
Keero Birla
Peter Buddle
Jennifer Chew
Durga Polashi
Chew-Bose
Anirban Choudhury
Subir Das
Kiran Dholakia
Lisa Foster
Mark Krupa
Rose Nolan
Mazhar Rafi Qureshi
Himmat Shinhat
Jaspreet Singh
Vasu Seshadri

Lighting Design	Brent Dinsmore
Set Design	Mark Buntrock
Song Lyrics	Rana Bose
Music Composer	Himmat Shinhat
Sound Track	Himmat Shinhat, Rana Bose
Creative Consultant & Associate Director	Andy Calamatas
Costumes	Lisa Foster & Rana Bose
Director	Rana Bose

Scene 1

Jazz riff in the blackout. Solo sax player comes slowly into view, playing in a Montreal bar. As he finishes, warm applause. As lights slowly come up, some people are seen leaving. Sparse but modern bar. Minimal furniture. Bartender Jack, big guy, chats with everybody, knows them by name. Switches on large-screen TV. Hockey game, 1989 Stanley Cup play-offs is on. In a dark corner sits Mr Paul DeCosta, the former carpet dealer, and present owner of this bar, quietly observing everybody, reading a paper. There is a man talking to DeCosta, who often goes over and uses the phone. There may be two other young people sitting at the bar. There is another man sitting at a table and reading. This is Prof. Amit Bose. Two tables and chairs upstage. The sound track is located through stereo speakers, throughout the audience, so that the sounds of the bar are also coming from the audience. A young woman, Anita, is reading a book with great interest. She whips out a notebook and starts writing something very thoughtfully. Sometimes she looks around the bar. Her friend Gene carries on watching the game, having fries and beer

ANITA. Gene, look at this . . . look at this. Will you quit watching the game . . . (*She slaps him on the wrist.*)

GENE. What? . . . What? (*She prevents him from watching the game. He gives up after a while, stretches and laughs at her.*) Just a minute!

ANITA. Look at this . . . look at this picture of this bar in St Antoine Street, 1928. St Antoine Street . . . Just like the inside of this one.

GENE. Antoine . . . not Anto anne . . .

ANITA. OK, whatever . . . Listen to this. St Antoine used to have the hottest jazz clubs in the city. Black musicians . . . in their own clubs. Right here . . . at this corner . . . this club, this very club could have been one of the top jazz clubs in the thirties. (*She looks up towards the ceiling.*)

GENE. OK! OK! Everybody knows that. Will you let me watch this . . . Everybody knows Montreal was swing city, at that time.

Everybody was getting out of the scene at New York, from prohibition, and heading for Montreal!

ANITA (*reads and as she reads, her friend, Gene mocks her by mimicking whatever she reads*). Listen to this concise bit of historiography. 'A city founded by the Iroquois Nation, where now stands the Ville Marie expressway, gave way to waves of settlers, first from New France, then the Irish who settled at the Point. Most black people who were already here for several centuries and were hired to work on the railway lines, lived along the ridge, in the St. Henri district.

. . .Stop it . . . As new waves of settlers came, the white-well-to-do inhabitants, moved up the ridge to the top of the hill . . . I said stop . . . But when it came to entertainment at night, they would drop over the ridge and come crawling down to where the action was. All along the railroad lines of St Antoine, heading upto Windsor Station, were jazz spots frequented by big names from New York and all over. The remnants of some of these nightspots are still visible along the expressway. The night's entertainment meant underground crap halls, girlie shows on Bishop Street, prostitution. Sin city was on the build. And along with it came gangs . . . cut it out . . . Gangs that controlled all traffic along the railway lines. . . . Must have been some other time . . . (*She hesitates and waits for a while.*). Striking. It's striking, Gene. (*Bartender listens in on conversation, amused.*)

GENE. What? What's striking . . .

ANITA. Never mind. The ridge. That's what I meant. The railway lines below and the gentry along St Jacques and the Upper Lachine Road . . . Do railway lines always separate the . . .

GENE. Hey! The ridge . . . has a name . . . did you know that?

ANITA. Yes, of course . . . it is mentioned here in this book . . . hang on . . . here . . . It was called the Sulpician Escarpment.

GENE. Right. The Sulpician Escarpment. If you step out and look towards the west, you will see a very ugly dome, a little way towards the south. It is called St. Cunegonde's Church, built by the Sulpician order.

JACK. Montreal landmark, bud . . . call it ugly and you'll get a lot of people real sore.

GENE. Just a matter of time (*repeats*) . . . before Dore hands it over to some developer . . .

JACK. Uh! Uh! Not that. Too much history . . . to it. Dore does that and he's gonna be history himself . . . the rest of his party gonna walk out on him.

ANITA. But why is it called the Sulpician Escarpment, though? It's a fault line. It should have a geological sounding name. It's a ridge formed by . . . (*One of the last remaining men in the bar leaves.*)

GENE. That's what it is. It's a cliff, Anita . . . a long cliff . . . that separates . . .

JACK. . . . the bottom of Montreal from the top.

ANITA. But the name . . .?

JACK. . . . A political fault line, that's what it is, bud . . . it's been like that. Now let me tell you, that Prof. who just left, he knows all about it . . . if you're up on top, you can't see the bottom. And the further up on the hill you go, the less you see over the ridge. The slope is gentle. And the monks . . . the Sulpecese you know what I mean . . . got the Mohawks to move out to Kahnawake . . . that was the first move. And then everybody who has moved in, has had to move out. First came the factories, then the CN lines, then the expressway and the development. Wave after wave.

GENE. Hey, come to think of it! This piece of Montreal, which you are in right now, could very well be a landmark site. Right Jack? Man! Look at the ceiling. (*He gets up and walks around.*)

DECOSTA (*puts his paper down*). It is a landmark. It's to be declared a heritage site, very soon.

JACK (*winks*). Huh! The boss done his homework, awright.

GENE. Tell me Mr DeCosta, how'd you land this prime piece of estate. I mean, it must have cost a fortune. Just look at it! With all the other developers . . . fighting for a chance to lay their paws on it. I heard the Reichmans were eyeing this for a while.

JACK. This is his fourth spot in the city, bud. Man's been around.

(Mr DeCosta signals the other man in the bar, who was sitting at the bar with his back to the audience. They leave without notice.)

GENE. Say, Mr DeCosta ! When can we chat . . . God! I'd love to do a piece, you know. These walls are reeking with jazz and intrigue . . . Man! This could be the very spot where Kenny Rockhead hid out during his bootleg days, before he opened up his spot.

ANITA. He's gone, Gene!

GENE. I know.

ANITA. I meant Mr DeCosta.

GENE. Hey! Where'd he go. Fuckin' slimedog. (*Runs out after him and then returns.*) Can never get him to talk, man!

JACK. Kid, let me tell ya something. (*Signals to come closer.*) You don't mess with this cat. When I say he's been around, I mean it. OK? You don't do your journalism crap on him. I told you before. He is shy. Period.

GENE. I ain't shy! Why should I? I've been looking for a lead to do a piece on the neighbourhood—and . . . he just won't give. Why? Man, I been hanging around here for the dope on him, like a vulture, you know what I mean? It's gonna get him more clientele. It's slack time . . . he can only benefit . . .

JACK. Boy, are you desperate and stubborn! . . . There's no story here! Look, if you want some interesting gossip come on Thursday nights. That McGill prof comes and sits down right there, every Thursday. Knows more about the history of this joint, than my boss . . .

ANITA. But, why is DeCosta so uptight?. . .Why does he get up and leave . . . Every time he opens his mouth, it's like, he realizes he's gone too far and he slinks away.

GENE. Yeah, right! Shuts up and splits like a bat, man. Has he got something against me? Lookit . . . here's a guy . . . comes to Canada from the black hole, Calcutta . . . selling carpets to Montreal . . . and twenty years later . . .

JACK. He's still here . . . in another hole . . . (*smiles to himself*).

GENE. Make a great story, man. Put him on the map. Right next to Rockhead . . . or Steep . . . Steep Wade. Just did a piece on him. Hey, chief! Ever heard of Steep Wade? Went to school right here in Montreal, at the Strathern High on Jeanne Mance street . . . took him nine years to do seven grades . . . so he quit school and picked up the alto . . . didn't work out too good . . . so he picks up the reeds—and guess what! He was the first man to play bebop regularly in Montreal, at the Cafe St Michel, right here on St Anto-anne!

JACK . . . Hey! you, fuckin' motormouth, shut up and listen to me. I'm gonna tell you'll something, 'cos the lady here is writing her thesis in history . . .

ANITA. Urban Anthropology . . . Jack.

JACK. Right, that's what I meant . . . and that's OK, but you, you are nosy . . . lookin' for a story . . . you wanna check into the past, the buildings, the bricks, the streets . . . that's OK, but you don't nose into people's lives, now . . . and the boss don't like you . . . and he's told me that . . .

GENE. Which means I should come here more often.

JACK. You come here as much as you want but don't do your whiny front page ethnic developer story . . . on him.

ANITA. Jack, you didn't answer my question. What's he so uptight about?

JACK. Ma'am, the boss's been here so long, he knows the hides of everybody who came with him and after. And if he ain't telling anybody anything, that's 'cos he got nothing to tell you. If you wanna write a story, bud, write it down now. I'll tell you. He made an honest living selling carpets and then the Kashmir carpets got done for cheap in China, or Persia or somewhere else. So now he doesn't import carpets. He's moved into prime property. From carpets to bars. Not rags to riches. Carpets to bars. End of story. That exciting enough for your dimwit paper?

GENE. Fix me a scotch, Jack. I'll go to the john. (*He leaves.*)

JACK. I'll fix you nothing. I'm closing. It's almost two.

GENE (*from outside*). Hey, I pay for what I drink. Does DeCosta have a problem with that, or is that being nosy too . . .

JACK. The lady here goes to school. She ought to go home. You don't, I know. Probably never did!

ANITA. Honestly, Jack, why does Mr DeCosta keep such a low profile? Every time we come here, he disappears . . . after a while.

JACK. I don't really know. All's I sense, and I've been with him five years now . . . he's got a deep grudge. You know what I mean. Against nosy folks. Drop by sometime, without your friend, and we will chat. There are other cats, who come here all the time. Much more interesting. Tell your friend, he can do a story on them, get a scoop . . . you know, that way he'd be fishing in deeper waters, as the saying goes . . . lay the bait on the big time stuff. You got MPs, MNAs, you got lobbyists, entertainers, you got cops in mufti, you got McGill profs drunk on their butts, hatching plots against each other . . . what more does he want? There's more juice there without Paul. Tell him to leave Paul alone. (*Train sound is heard in the distance . . .*)

Fade into . . .

Scene 2.

Flashback. Anita seems restless, sitting under a dim light on the same bar stool. Staring out. Lights dim and suddenly the TV screen flickers and changes to the sound of a rapidly moving train as it whizzes by. 1968. Calcutta, India. Light effects. Simultaneously, the sounds of a scuffle, a murderous scream, abusive epithets, all in the dark. Anita is staring into the scene. Somebody has been murdered and the only lights are those from the passing train's window lights. The victim collapses, gurgling blood. The train sound fades away and a man with a particularly heavy pair of boots walks towards the audience. Two other men, one with a rod, sneak away from behind him. His face is not visible, because of a hat he is wearing. He picks out a kerchief from his pocket and cleans the blade of a sharp stiletto-like knife, covered in blood. As he wipes the blood, he whistles a familiar tune (like 'Tequila'). He turns around and looks at the corpse before he walks away.

MAN. Fucking bastard! Wanna clean up the joint ? (*Walks away mumbling.*) Change the world, eh? Schmuck!

Sound track picks up 'Tequila'. Lights spread and upstage right is a country liquor store, in Calcutta. Sign says 'Kasba Star Flying Club'. A man stands behind a window with a grill. Bottles in shelves behind him. He is the bartender. In front of the window, one table with a few benches. Two guys are drunk and twisting away to 'Tequila' as it is being played through a small radio in the bar. Music stops. Radio man announces end of music programme, local news to follow.

MAN 1 (*spitting out booze*). Sheeet! Fuck the news, man! Fuck the news. Screw it, I said. (*Both sit down, for a second.*)

MAN 2. Yeah, screw it. Yeah! (*Climbs up on a bench*) All Indira Radio. Today Mrs Gandhi opened a school for the blind. Tomorrow she will travel to Yugoslavia, to represent mother India in a non-aligned summit. Day after tomorrow Mrs Gandhi will . . .

MAN 1. . . . she will take a shit on behalf of the nation . . . (*both start laughing*).

BARTENDER. Hey! You! Shut up! OK? It's my bar and my radio.

MAN 1. Shhhh!

Radio. 'This is All India Radio, Calcutta. Here are the highlights of the local news today. US Defence Secretary Robert McNamara, on his way home from Vietnam, made a brief stopover at Calcutta today. Mr McNamara had to be flown by helicopter from Calcutta Airport to the Governor's House, because of reported attempts by radical extremists to dynamite a flyover on the highway leading into the city. Mr McNamara appeared unaware of the incident. In local news today, a well-known extremist leader with known affiliation to criminal gangs operating in the railway yards in the Kasba area of southern Calcutta was found brutally stabbed to death in an alley adjacent to the railway lines. His death, according to the police, was a result of a fallout between rival gangs. No arrests have been made. The murder weapon was not found, although the police did confirm that the victim was disembowelled' . . . *Bartender shuts off radio.*

MAN 1. Ai . . . ai . . . ai, ai . . . a . . . (*grips his stomach and rolls over in mock pain*).

MAN 2. Disembowelled! You mean, . . . it's a murder and not a harakiri, this time? Very strange . . . Boss . . .very strange . . .

MAN 1. This is something new . . . boss . . . death due to gang-warfare! (*He swallows*) . . . Montuda, what is happening to the joint . . . out of control, man . . .

BARTENDER. . . . Out of control is right . . . how 'bout paying up? I tell you, next time, no dough, no booze. House rules. OK? No credit.

MAN 1. Boss, have we ever gone away without paying? You are the only boss we have! (*Salutes*) We are jobless, but not bossless! *Sala*, you are the boss of booze! (*Blows a kiss.*)

BAR. Yeah! Right! You . . . you have not paid for the last two weeks . . . and the total is now . . . let me see . . . Rs 98. What do you think . . . this bar is run by the Sisters of Charity?

MAN 2. Boss, who do you think killed the boy?

BAR. How do I know? And if I knew, why would I tell you . . . next thing you'll be singing to the cops . . .

man 1. Hey, Montuda, don't insult us, man. We are 'line people', you know what I mean?

BAR. Yeah, tell me what you mean! Line people, hah!

MAN 1. Line people don't do petty stuff like spying for the pigs, ratting on the people. OK? Call me a thief . . . that's OK, call me a bum . . . that's OK . . . but don't call me a police spy. Two things I don't do . . . go whoring and spy for the cops . . . OK?

BAR. Oh, shut up! I'm gonna close down now . . . and I got no time for your pious shit. Next week you put the cash down first, then you stick your hand in the cage.

MAN 2. Montuda, this business is getting serious . . . one after the other, like flies, they are killing these college boys . . . every night . . .

MAN 1. Yeah . . . thai . . . thai . . . thai (*feigns pointing a pistol*).

BAR. You noticed, huh? Getting hooked into politics? Are you?. . . Huh! . . . This one was a biggie, though. They won't catch the killer . . . 'cos the bird has flown, gone . . . into the sky. But they would have a hard time covering this one up. The Company, my friend . . .

MAN 1. Why do they need to cover up? They have been killing the boys every day . . . and nobody says a word . . .

BAR. Because the kid was famous . . . top student. The father was a big shot lawyer . . . big guns.

MAN 2. Boss, word is out that this time the SB, Special Branch, was called in to do the job. Not ordinary beat cops . . . because those motherfuckers always screw up.

MAN 1. Yeah. Last time they shot this other boy with a 38 and said the boy had committed suicide because of a love affair.

MAN 2. Then they changed the story. When some journalists asked how come he was shot in the back with a Smith & Wesson, which only sergeants carry.

MAN 1. Yeah . . . fuck . . . normally if you wanna do suicide . . . you poof (*points to his head and then struggles to point to his back*).

MAN 2. Then they said it was an encounter with the cops. The kid had tried to grab a gun from the cops, and in the scuffle . . .

MAN 1. Yeah, yeah, yeah . . . Boss, if the boy's father was such a big shot lawyer, why doesn't he push somebody at the federal level?

BAR. He has.

MAN 1. And . . .

BAR (*gap*). . . . it's too late, the bird has flown . . . big bird . . . big company . . . no trace . . . gone . . . into the sky . . . (*Lights fade . . . spot on bar . . . bird wings sound switches to the reverberation of a 'copter—very loud*) . . . The weapon was so deadly . . . Like the claws of an eagle . . . It ripped his guts out and left them out in the sewer in a heap . . . and . . . there was a special angle to the blade . . . fifteen degrees from the tip down. Very rare piece . . . that angle . . . You cannot get that knife here . . .

Lights fade out on country liqour store and switch back to Montreal bar. Anita comes out of her flashback frame.

ANITA. Good night, Jack. I'll be over to talk to you. One of these nights.

She leaves. Heard in the corridor 'Gene , let's go . . . bar's closed. Forget it . . .' As soon as they leave, lights start dimming. Mr DeCosta comes back. The other man also leaves, wishing DeCosta on his way out . . . DeCosta starts asking Jack questions very agitatedly.

MR DECOSTA. What'd you tell him? What'd he want?

JACK. Nothing, Paul . . . nothing.

DECOSTA. He is a nosy motherfucker . . . she's OK. I don't mind her. She's OK. But he's curious, the sonofabitch.

JACK. Paul, someday, you gotta straighten your papers out, man. I mean, how long are you gonna carry on like this? Constantly a nervous wreck, man. Just walk up to immigration and tell 'em your story . . . they won't kick you out. If I were them I'd have a good laugh. On a three-week visa, you stayed on for twenty years . . . and they still can't figure it out . . . Twenty years and you still don't have papers. Man!

DECOSTA. Jack . . . I've told you many times. You keep your lips shut tight about me and I keep the lid on you. OK? I like you and I treat you right, let's keep it that way.

Both stare at each other for a while. Silence.

JACK. You gonna close?

DECOSTA. Yup.

JACK. OK! I'll see you tomorrow. Catch a few winks, man.

Mr DeCosta sits down and the lights go off slowly on him, top down.

Scene 3

Jet sounds. International Airport, Montreal. Airport announcement, announces the arrival of luggage from KLM flight 062 from Amsterdam on Carousel 5. On a riser or on a mezzanine type level, there is the Immigration booth. Line up of passengers. Three Indian-looking people are visible, amongst others. Two are in line, one comes a little later. At the Montreal bar, under very dim blue lights, one can see Anita talking to Jack. Their entire conversation goes on while the airport scene is also going on at another level of the stage. Their conversation can barely be heard. Jack is swigging down a few, while talking to her. In the beginning he is quite cool and collected. She cajoles him. Towards the end he loses it and becomes increasingly audible. She corners him gradually—to the point that she goes over the bar and straight for him. This is like a story being told by Jack.

IMMIG. Next. Your name, please.

DECOSTA (*seems very hurried*). Mr Paul DeCosta. Good afternoon, sir. I am an Indian citizen on business.

IMMIG. What is the length of your stay in Canada?

DECOSTA. Two weeks, maximum.

IMMIG. What is the nature of your business?

DECOSTA. I am importing carpets into Canada.

IMMIG. You have three weeks on your visa, single entry, non-renewable. Next. (*Jack laughs out loud at this point and Anita says 'For three weeks only . . .?'*)

DECOSTA (*looks around*). My card sir, in case . . .

IMMIG. Next . . .

A woman is next . . . quickly the passport is stamped and she leaves. Standing behind is Mr Chatterjee, very suave and confident-looking.

CHAT. Good afternoon. My name is Animesh Chatterjee. Ace Chatterjee for short. My passport is Indian. I have permanent resident status in Canada.

IMMIG. Are you alone?

CHAT. For the time being . . . my wife will follow.

IMMIG. How much money are you bringing into Canada?

CHAT. Not much. About $1000.

IMMIG (*looks up*). And what are your plans with $1000?

CHAT. I am a professional engineer. (*Lot of confidence and arrogance*) I have a job offer from Energy Consultants of Canada Inc. ECC on Dorchester Avenue, corner of Rue Guy. Here. All the particulars are there.

IMMIG. When does the passport expire? Ah! It's a brand new passport. Expires on . . . December 4th, 1979. (*He picks up a phone and speaks softly for a while, with his back to the audience.*) You see the officer on that side. He will advise you of the next step.

CHAT. Is there a problem?

IMMIG. Next.

Next, a white person. Quiet, conversation. Mr Chatterjee stomps around for a while, hissing under his breath, finally finds the room, where he is supposed to go and leaves.

IMMIG. Next.

BOSE. Hi!

IMMIG (*looks at his papers*). You have come to study . . . at McGill. Also from India. Lots of Indians today, eh? From Calcutta.

BOSE. Two before me, yes.

IMMIG. Do you have any gifts or presents?

BOSE. No sir, I don't know anybody here. I am here to do my Master's and then I will go back.

IMMIG. Go into that booth and they will advise you about health requirements.

BOSE. Thank you, sir.

IMMIG. Next.

Immediately lights fade. Sound track has a sound of birds fluttering away. Lights start fading—Jack gets louder and louder . . .

JACK. Thank me . . . schmuck, thank me . . . That's it. That's it. I've told you more than I've told anybody, ever. Jesus! And I thought that punk friend of yours was nosy . . .

ANITA. So you knew Bose from before, but how did you know the rest?

JACK. Because of Paul. Paul led me to my first job in Montreal and he told me . . . And why do I have to tell you, goddammit? Why do you care . . . (*He smashes a glass onto the floor in a rage.*) And besides that was then . . . and this is now. That's it. I turned a leaf! OK! End of story . . . For twenty years I've shut up about it and you had to wring it out. And tell that friend of yours . . . there's nothing for him here . . .

ANITA. Don't worry . . . (*He looks away. Anita starts moving away from him like a panther, like she has made up her mind. She leaves the bar and comes and stands under a sharp overhead spot. Dark shadows on her face . . . Next scene starts at the Calcutta country liquor store immediately.*)

Scene 4

Anita's flashback. She is witnessing this scene. Back in the same country liquor store, only one man is there. Drunk. Face down on the table. Bartender is cleaning glasses. Lights slowly light up the doorway. A woman and a young girl are standing at the entrance.

BAR. Come, dear . . . come in. I know who you are. (*He comes from behind the window and asks them to sit down.*)

Hey Footo, disappear, man—quick. Out. Split, I said.

Footo (MAN 1) *wakes up, disoriented, and then leaves. On his way out he sees the woman and child and is heard screaming* 'Sala, *the bird has flown, brother . . . gone . . . the bird has flown'. He screams and there is the sound of a woman somewhere else in the alley shouting back: 'Oy, Footo shut the fuck up, man . . . and go home . . .' Footo: 'Yeah, yeah . . . going, going gone home . . .'. Sound of crash against garbage cans . . . Mother and child are startled and look towards the exit.*

WOM. I was told . . . you knew my boy.

BAR. Yes, I had seen him a few times.

WOM (*looks around*). Did he come here often?

BAR. Once in a while, my dear. But not really to drink. You know, how he was. He hung out with everybody . . . pimps, crooks, thugs, pickpockets, domestics, mill-workers, the ladies . . . yes, you name it—please sit down, can I get you some orange juice?

WOM. No, thank you.

BAR. Yes, your son . . . ready to sort out everybody's problem. You know, and don't believe what the papers say about him. That is all police talk. When they want to bump off someone—they spread nonsense. Make it look like a gang hit.

WOM. I was told that you know the person who killed my boy.

He motions her to sit down and then speaks with a lowered voice in the beginning.

BAR. Not too much. This was a very top level hit, ma'am. Top level. Nothing to do with the gangs here. From what I've heard from the boys. They tell me, there was a detective officer who carried it out. Orders from the very top.

WOM. A police officer? But they killed him with a knife!

BAR. Not just a knife, ma'am. A very deadly knife . . . The whole affair was pre-planned. Maybe for months. The Company . . .

WOM: Pre-planned?

BAR. Made to look like a gang hit. But I have no names. If I knew, I would let you know. But I tell the kids who come here—the bird has flown, ma'am. Gone. (*The young girl stares at him suddenly.*)

WOM. What do you mean by that?

BAR. It is too late, now. Your husband is a famous man. They had to cover it up and make it look like a gang hit . . .

WOM. But what does that . . . my boy had left home almost two years ago . . .

BAR. Let me explain this to you. This ghetto's been run by the parties. Different parties at different times and their gangsters, with the cops in the shadows.

WOM. I have heard that.

BAR. From day one, your boy didn't give a damn for all this and stepped all over their toes. All the old slum lords had never seen anything like this. In one month, your boy had shaken up their power base. Made them nervous wrecks. Oh, yes.

WOM. But then didn't some of the people here want to stand by him, sir . . . Was it that difficult?

BAR. Stand by? Ma'am. Let me tell you something. They say still waters run deep. Here the water flows. Nothing runs deep. The tragedy is he was liked by everybody, but tomorrow he will be forgotten, because he had politics. They had none. For them it was great while he was around. Tomorrow is a new day, a new hero. (*He walks back to the bar . . . and fetches a glass.*) I never drink on the job. Against my religion.

But the bar is shut for tonight. (*He brings his drink back and sits close to her.*)

BAR. For young men like your son, anything could be changed. No rules were sacred. But it's not true! The cops can slam the door on anybody . . . anytime . . . in fact, for your boy the doors were slammed shut all along.

WOM. My son believed . . .

BAR. In ideals? (*He smiles a little.*) Long time back someone somewhere said . . . all good things must come to an end. Like the dip in the sine wave. All lessons are lost. We are approaching that point again. All ideals will be lost. And we will all have to start relearning again. From scratch. Point Zero.

WOM. Montuda . . . is that what they call you?

BAR. Yes, something like that . . . or when they are pissed they call me boss . . . behind my back they say 'fucking Jew'. I'm half-jew, you know. Baghdadi. From the famous Sassoon line. Lost tribe. I'm the only one, left, in Calcutta. I think, anyway . . . Mordechai Sassoon. That's what my father called me. And these kids call me Montu. Big brother Montu . . . dispenser of home-made paradise. Bubbly from the heavens. (*Silence for a while. The young girl moves to centrestage.*)

WOM. Please, Montuda . . . do you have any names? You must know something more?

BAR. The Company, ma'am. Big job.

The lights started fading out. The young girl is standing at down stage centre. Only spot on her. She is staring out.

WOM. The Company? Please, Montuda, can you tell me who took my boy away? You must know something. They said you can help, sir.

BAR. It's very late, ma'am. There is too much trouble in the ghetto these days.

WOM. But they said that you had some leads. I know I can never get him back. But, please . . . I want to know? Why did they do that to my boy? Tore his guts out, Montuda. They tore his guts out.

BAR. I will walk you to your car. If I hear something . . .

They get up and start leaving. They stop and turn around to see the young girl still staring out. Train sound in the distance. Lights fade.

Scene 5

Scene starts with a video pan along Fort Street at night as we enter the ramp to the 20. Goes on and settles down with a top view of the ridge from the Upper Lachine Road and then fades out. Gene and Anita both sitting away from each other, probably on a park bench, at the edge of the escarpment. Dry leaves on the ground. He fidgets, lights a cigarette. Slowly the backdrop lights up, as if it is a top view of the city at night. Some silence. Once they start speaking there is a strain of a tune that drifts in and out.

GENE. Let's get to the point . . . It's not like I don't know what you are after . . .

ANITA (*suddenly*). No, no, no! You don't know what I am after . . . but it's not important, it does not make me any different from anybody else, that you may have known before . . .

GENE. How do you know who I have known before?

ANITA. I mean in a generic sense!

GENE. So, you're lumping all my genre together in one heap . . . And yet, I say, you are different. (*Silently stares at her.*) You know what, your eyes! They wander, when I am . . .

ANITA. Jesus! Can we stop this . . .

GENE. Stop what . . .?

ANITA. This long distance fucking . . .

GENE. Distance? Right, distance! There is a distance in your eyes, that jumps in between and I lose you completely. (*She ignores him for a while.*) Like you are listening, not hearing? Are you listening, now?

ANITA. Yes, I'm listening, I am . . . and . . . believe me, but my limbs are tired . . . Gene . . . they cannot see beyond this ridge. They cannot see beyond this ridge. Everything beyond is blurred.

GENE. Why can't you see beyond the ridge . . . What is with this Sulpician Escarpment? . . . And you don't see with your limbs, anyway . . . with limbs you cover distances . . . you hold on . . . you criss-cross . . . you walk over . . .

ANITA. Exactly . . . and yet you say there is distance in my eyes . . . (*She comes closer to him . . . and puts her arms through his and embraces him.*) Is this distance?

GENE. What I mean is . . .

ANITA. . . .What you mean is . . . I am not warming up to you . . . not having corresponding notions . . . not getting excited about your stories . . .

GENE. Wait a minute . . . (*He moves away.*) Don't treat me in such a cavalier fashion. Yes, corresponding emotions, but not the way you think it is. Suddenly as we go along, something happens . . . There is a crispness in the air, between us . . .

ANITA. Ah! look at your metaphors. Crispness! Dry leaves strewn all over. We are already in the autumn of our thing, is it? Is it thing or is it fling? And besides, look at her! She is not outgoing. She is from another world. Where things are done slower, less frequently, with less gusto . . . she must be approached with caution . . . eastern way. . . (*She sits down on the bench cross-legged, and closes her eyes . . . smiling.*)

GENE (*walks up to her, almost like he is going to put his arms around her, from behind. Then stops*). What the fuck! Don't do this to me. Do you think I am just beating around the bush for the physical thing. The togetherness, the . . .

ANITA. No, no! You like me—the little intrigue, here and there . . . but mostly you admire my head. Up here. I know it. And I'll make it easier . . . I'm the one that is passionate as hell . . . and you're the one who controls . . .

GENE. Can I do my own thinking?

ANITA. . . . and walks on the edge . . . and I don't think you are unleashing yourself on an unsuspecting foreign student—insecure and unsure as she is, sitting on the edge of this big city—an innocent female, engaged in intense anthropological research on . . .

GENE. . . . on bar life and jazz in the post-depression era, where the city's architecture and urban migration intrigue her so much that no other conversation can light up her eyes, other than that. (*She laughs.*) And for that she is willing to hang around in some of the lowliest dives in the city, in the wee hours of the morning. Tell me, is she collecting oral history samples of local folk lore or . . .?

(*Anita pulls him towards her.*) How deep have you delved, ma'am, into the intriguing history of our fair city? Do you have enough material for your thesis . . . What use can I be for you?

ANITA (*starts laughing quite loudly, then stops, looks suddenly at him.*) This is borderline rudeness. But carry on, it does not bother me. If I didn't trust you, I wouldn't be here . . . Yes, I need you. I need you and I do not have to explain it. Because explaining only drags in the past. . . for which you have no flavour.

GENE. I am sorry. Anita, I am talking about silence about the past. Silence about our lives. This is the first time we are talking about all this. I've known you a year. And I know nothing about you. I'm talking about the unsaid word. And I don't want you to belittle me. I want to talk to you.

ANITA. I thought that was the idea of coming here and not going to Ben's.

GENE (*after some silence*). We are like silent dunes in a desert. I want to bridge the gap between the dunes, the noiseless stretches—the uncensored exchanges, which I know mean something else to you. They must. And yet you won't let me in on them. You know what I mean? That is the crispness I'm talking about. So, I know what you want and you know what I want. And I can operate better. That's it.

ANITA. So what would you like to do about it?

GENE. What would I like to do?. . . I would like to . . .

ANITA. Say it . . . Tell me what you would like to do . . . I'm not unprepared . . . and I know, like me, you are also searching . . . and I hope for god's sake you don't beat around . . .

GENE. First of all, I am not a careerist rat, scrambling for fame and fortune in this city's withering print medium. 'By any means necessary'. Isn't that what you said the other day?

ANITA. I've heard that said about you . . . that you are a ferocious journalist, you will bite anything . . . but I do not believe it.

GENE. Yet, you must have me . . .

ANITA. Have you? You make it sound like . . .

GENE. Around . . . Have me around. That's what I meant . . .

ANITA. But I want to have you. Can I? Do you understand that! I do not have to explain that . . . do I? Why do we have to explain everything like it must fit into one whole personality? Can I be . . .

GENE. What I am saying is that I must accompany you and yet you will never say it. And what is it that must make this fruitful, eventful, fulfilling and exciting for me, or am I being a stupid, juvenile, pestilential white male hankering for your hyperintellectual Asian id. I mean, tell me, what is it that you are really after?

ANITA. Why? Men! . . . Men! Don't you see? I'm after men!

GENE (*walks around for a while, looks at her, thinking*). So, I must wait, still . . . while you hold close to yourself . . . something that only you must know . . . I must wait . . . because you will not really share that special corner of your mind . . . and I must wait, while you avoid issues and do ballet on the edge of the Escarpment . . . the fucking Escarpment . . . most people in Montreal don't even know about it!

ANITA. I asked you what was it that you would like to do most . . . with your life . . .

GENE. The Escarpment . . . it's like a ridge that separates two worlds, between the past and now, between those up there and those below . . . and between you and me. . . differences installed, not natural.

ANITA. You didn't answer. . . let me explain something to you . . . please . . . at the present time we are two people . . . young . . . who are loitering around each other . . . and indefiniteness bothers you . . . because you would like to sit down and write a conclusion . . . as in your articles . . . for the paper . . . an ending . . . you are determined that life must be allocated into slots and you must make that allocation of love, life and career systematically, now! That's your frame, right?

GENE. Close, but too clinical.

ANITA. Yes, clinical because . . . all frames must conform . . . the pressures are heavy but . . . nevertheless, you are hip and modern . . . words like commitment do not slip from your lips—so what you would like to hear is some sort of an ordered reason and rationale for whatever you must do . . .

GENE. My rationale for doing things is obvious . . . yes, I must make my existence work for me. Not weigh me down. I must be excited and productive—my energies must flow all the time . . . I must produce at a given time and reap the benefits of that production at another time . . . sit back, relax, and then get back again to work like crazy . . . but I must not be so automatic, right? . . . That's why I . . .

ANITA. Hang out with me!

GENE. And there is nothing mercenary about that. I am not exoticizing you . . . I am not intrigued by you . . . wait a minute, I am. Yes. I must know what's next . . . Anita, I must know, what is the next piece in the puzzle . . .

ANITA. What's next on my hit list . . .?

GENE. Yes, what is it? Even though you make it awfully ominous!

At this point, the sound of a train is heard and its approaching lights. The little girl from the first scene, with her back to the audience is seen staring out at the passing train, at a raised level. Either by video projection or lights. Anita starts backing out and disappears. Gene is left alone, talking to himself.

I have to know, what is it that makes you dig deeper and deeper into this little stretch of the world . . . so far away from yours, I mean what is the connection, why do trains intrigue you, what are you looking for goddammit, and why must I hang around . . . now don't say it . . . don't say it . . . it is my choice, I know . . . but you have ensured that I must be there to be a witness, to what? I goddam have no idea . . . you don't tell me to stay and yet I know I must . . . it's not just the attraction of being your friend . . . I am almost ensnared in an intrigue only you can look into . . . not me . . . you are challenging me to be more curious, yet you won't let me in . . . (*He bends down to sit and notices she is gone.*) Anita . . . Anita . . .

Jazz riff . . . floats in.

Scene 6

Upstage right. Gene the reporter is typing away furiously on a laptop. Only a table and a chair under a sharp spot. At some point he gets up and starts talking to the audience, occasionally reading from a piece of paper. Music track continues softly for a while. As he introduces each character, in his monologue, they appear almost as props to aid the process, under sharp spots.

GENE. Reliable sources in the Asian community . . . let's call my mole Sid Krishna for the time being . . . tell me that on the 15th of March 1969—the ides, my friend—three people disembarked from a plane at Dorval Airport. None of them knew each other, then. All stepped onto a new soil to make a new beginning. They had all come from India, directly, changing planes at Amsterdam, Schipol Airport. Twenty years later they have all met each other and they are all doing very well, thank you. Moneywise, that is. By Indian standards, not all respectably. The first, Mr Paul DeCosta, owns a string of bars. Tight lipped man. Can't squeeze a word out of him. His barman, Jack Simard, says 'Leave him alone. Don't mess with him. He's been around.' Whatever the hell that means. He is a quiet, observant but occasionally nervous man who listens in on all conversations at his bar. No family, no known relatives. As if he had no past. Jack protects his boss, like between them they share nasty secrets about each other. What is the score here? Hey! I don't know. But I'll find out!

Next comes Professor Amit Bose. Amiable Amit. Arrived on the same plane with Paul DeCosta and a regular at his bar. But a totally different personality. Quiet, unassuming man. Fits perfectly into the description of a subalternist historian, which is history from below, my friend. Subaltern. History of the dispossessed. Said in the language of the insurgent, but said with dignity and flawlessly. Draws a large class every semester. Brilliant fellow, he also specializes in Montreal history. Montreal history, did I say? Yes! My main man . . . he came here to do a Masters in Physics, switched over to Humanities. Finished a Ph.D. at McGill in record time. Now, he knows more about Montreal history than most curators in this city. Graeme Decarie included. Now, isn't that something else! Jack loves to chat about him. 'Cos the Prof supplies him with fresh gossip from McGill. Jack has radar for ears. He's soaked up so much in that 6.2 inches between his two ears, he could work undercover for any agency. And Prof Bose loves Jack. So what's the mystery, here? Just hold your horses!

Next. Third person on the plane. Mr Animesh Chatterjee. P.Eng. Professional Engineer. Smooth talking, high-flying, cocky, entrepreneur and a regular sonofabitch. Works twice as hard as an average Canadian, and makes it a point to let you know that he was in charge, the day he arrived on Canadian soil. Call him Ace. He likes it. No messing around with this dude. Recession? Never heard about it. Man's got construction contracts coming out of his ears. Not in Canada . . . but all over the world. And he's got connections. I mean connections. Let me jolt you with a few. Power Corp, Northern Telecom, Hydro-Quebec, SNC-Lavalin, ABB, Bechtel—you name it. He is walking in and out of their offices with contracts. Never heard about the bid process. What's his technique? Ah! Of that, later. And he is a big spender for one of the three federal parties. Which one, I don't know. But I'll find out. Can't be the NDP, for sure. Rumour is that the Caisse de Depot is interested in his moolah, too. And let me lay some protocol on you. He knows Ministers, secretaries and even some Premiers. He is in and out of the country every month. Goes to Europe, goes to Asia, every few months. Several projects in India. Knows big shots. He'll let you know how to do what, where with whom, and when. Like he says, he's got connections. Do this that way. Do that this way. Protocol. How do I know? Because I'm interested, man, I'm interested. Like Jack, the bartender says, I'm a nosy sonofabitch. I tell ya, I got something going here. I know. Maybe a real estate scam, maybe an inside deal on contracts, maybe a payoff involving mutual funds and the wife of a well-known MP, with a numbered account in the Islands! Who knows? But they all know each other and they all hang out at DeCosta's! Who knows? May also be a nice neighbourhood story, full of coincidences, jazz nostalgia, and local mystique. But I got a piece here, I know. Maybe a scoop . . . maybe a front-page leader . . .! Gotta work on it! That's all!

Plus, my girl Anita . . . another one, all the way from India, she's interested and she is the one who eggs me on. Why? Because shes got an avid interest in that region of Montreal,

St. Anto-anne, as she calls it, for her Master's thesis . . . At least that's what she says. Come to think of it, why is she interested in these three? One of them owns commercial real estate here, the other one knows the history of the joint and the third one hangs around in high places, to nail down contracts . . . Strange coincidence . . . and all of them flew in on the same bird twenty years ago from Amsterdam . . . I beg your pardon? Did I hear you say something? Excuse me, could you speak a bit louder . . . sir?

At this point, the lights suddenly go out and a tremendous scream is heard. Another violent murder. Behind a scrim, the Calcutta bartender is seen. He looks much older. He is screaming. 'Ha, ha, ha . . . sala, *I told you, I told you . . . the bird has flown, brother . . . the bird has flown . . . but wait a minute . . . it's not out of reach— not out of reach, brother . . . not out of reach . . .' As the lights come up slowly, a person is seen, exactly like the person in the first scene. His face is not visible. He is whistling the same tune as in the first scene. He wipes the blade of that same knife, carefully. Follow spot follows his feet out. As soon as he has left, Anita comes rushing in, towards Gene's table, screaming. He is sprawled on his desk. She comes rushing upto him and wakes him up.*

ANITA. Get up . . . Get up . . . Gene, get up!

GENE. What . . . What . . .? (*He grabs hold of her.*) What is it? Don't look so stupid? What is it?

ANITA. Jack . . . Jack was stabbed . . . last night!

GENE. What?

ANITA. With a stiletto . . . (*She is shaking.*)

GENE. You mean Jack Simard . . . at the bar?

ANITA. . . . His guts . . . were pulled out . . . Gene, he was dead before they got to the General. (*She sits down on the chair.*) Gene, I've gotto talk to you . . . This is terrible . . . what has happened? (*She is quiet for a while.*) I spoke to him last night for almost an hour. I can't believe this. (*He pulls out a drink for her. They start talking after a while.*)

GENE. You spoke to him last night? Why didn't you tell me you were there?

They look at each other.

ANITA. He told me a bunch of things . . .

GENE. When was that?

ANITA. It was early . . . before the crowds, and I left by the time it was seven. It got crowded.

GENE. When was he . . .?

ANITA. I don't know . . . but in the news they said it was around two in the morning.

GENE. Was there anybody you knew there?

ANITA. No, just DeCosta . . . and he left a few minutes after I arrived. Gene, there is something else.

GENE. What . . . the cops want to see me?

ANITA. No. But Jack asked me to warn you off. He said DeCosta didn't like the way you were nosing around. And that he had reason to be wary of you . . .

GENE. Me? Why? Unless he thought I was onto something . . .

ANITA. . . . And he said he could get pretty nasty. And he also told me he himself was thinking of splitting to Toronto. The joint was getting a bit seedy. Lately a bunch of guys were turning up and making it a rendezvous point.

GENE. Rendezvous point?

ANITA. He was not sure what it was all about. And here's the clincher. Paul DeCosta asked him to quit.

GENE. Jesus Christ! How come . . . you are leaving me out of all this . . . (*Whips around*) Is there something else that you are not telling me?

ANITA (*she is quiet for a while*). Gene, he told you . . . He didn't want to talk to you. But I knew there was something there for you . . . and I wanted to find out for you . . . and for myself. He asked me to see him, last night, alone.

GENE. You're leaving me out of all this . . . I don't understand, what's your angle, really. Are you doing field work for a thesis or . . . (*She rushes over and puts her hand over his mouth. They hold each other for a while.*)

GENE. I'm headin' out. I gotto take this up with the regulars there.

ANITA. Like who?

GENE. I don't know . . . but I'll find out.

ANITA. Hang on!

GENE. I bet I can from some of DeCosta's neighbours on the same strip. They go bar hopping. (*Gene puts on a jacket, lights a cigarette.*) You stay here tonight, I'll be back by ten. (*He rushes out. Anita is just about to say something, but stops.*)

ANITA. Somebody killed him with a knife. The knife had a steep angle to it. Fifteen degrees from the tip down. It's the kind of blade, which, when retracted, pulls the guts out with it.

She stares into the audience. As lights fade, one can barely hear footsteps coming closer. Anita puts her head down, and says 'God, what is happening!' As she says this, she gets up, looks at the audience and then, turning her back, slowly takes her shirt off. As she does this, a revolver drops to the ground. Gene is standing at the door, watching. She shudders. He comes forward slowly and holds her. Music.

Intermission.

Scene 7

Cocktails at the suburban house of Mr Ace Chatterjee. One tall lamp, one couch. A few seating arrangements. Ornate but tasteful. There is a waiter going around serving hors d'oevres and drinks. Present—Mr Chatterjee, Mrs Chatterjee, Prof. Amit Bose, Mr Paul DeCosta, Mr Jim Westman of Westman Associates. Mr DeCosta, sitting on the couch, a drink in his hand, looks distracted. There is an unfinished chess game on a table, that is occasionally being played by Chatterjee and Bose as they move around. Elevator music.

MRS CHAT (*laughs*). Absolutely, totally, flabbergasting. Is it not?

MR WESTMAN. What?

MRS CHAT. Jean Chretien's sentence construction! It seems like he is constructing his ideas, while he is constructing his sentences.

MR WESTMAN. Well! I wouldn't say that. He is walking on very familiar territory. Very experienced. The problem is that the political establishment has declared him a has-been. And that's his major handicap.

MRS CHAT. Well, but he always ends up saying things with a lot of gusto, eh? What a guy, though! He was over a few days ago, you know!

MR WEST. Was he? Well! Has Ace got something up his sleeve, there? Ha, Ha!

CHAT. I heard that! I heard that! But I tell you, Jim, Jean Chretien isn't my bag. Lots of heart, but no edge. You know what I mean! But he'll be the next PM. Mark my words.

BOSE. Check! (*Makes a move. Chatterjee is momentarily surprised.*)

MR WEST. Hey Ace, I heard you are off again, in the next few days—

CHAT. Yup . . . Off to China . . . How'd that happen now . . . Yes! China's where it's at . . .

WEST. China, eh? That country is going to be ecologically devastated at the pace they are going . . .

CHAT. Possibly. But they will come around. Like most other developing countries. The price of progress, as they say. Then we move on somewhere else (*makes a move*).

BOSE. You cannot do that (*points to his move*) . . .

CHAT. Oh, yes! I'm sorry . . . distracted. I need a refill (*gets up*).

MRS CHAT. Non-stop travelling. Non-stop. I tell him, get something here . . . like an establishment . . . you can run from Montreal . . . you know. One day here, next day there . . . today China . . . tomorrow Algeria . . . it's ridiculous . . . and the children have given up . . . I keep telling him get a stable operation here in Montreal . . . like Mr DeCosta.

BOSE. In Montreal? It's a mess.

WEST. Oh! No it isn't! Come on, Bose!

BOSE. There is no stability here. It's becoming a provincial capital—not an international city!

MRS CHAT. I know, isn't it terrible? Even the West Island malls are becoming drug joints. I see needles all over the place. There are girls soliciting openly! Massage parlours everywhere. Next thing, you know . . .

BOSE. Yes. But what I meant was all the economic hassles. Millions on UI. All the shelters are getting shut down. People are out on the street, mentally and physically, with nothing to lean on. No crutches.

MRS CHAT. Ah, but Amit, I don't understand. Why is it that welfare has become such an easy out. In our culture we would be—

BOSE. There are no jobs, Mrs Chatterjee—and today you need special skills, otherwise you're out on the street. No skills, no job.

WEST. So the taxes get higher, to fill the dole pot and beat the deficit, right?

BOSE. Wrong, the government must think long term. Spend money on training. Training is the key element. It has become very stylish to criticize the social safety net, as the main cause of the deficit.

WEST. Well, governments gotto lighten the load, you know.

BOSE. Everybody talks like they took Economics 101 from Ronald Reagan. And it's a shame, because Thatcher, Reagan, Mulroney and the rest of them have all disappeared, and they have left behind the legacy of states that don't care for the poor and the weak. Everybody fends for themselves . . .

MRS CHAT. Dog eats dog. I know what you mean! The other day . . .

BOSE. And it's not the financial crisis alone. Culturally also,

Montreal is becoming a satellite metropolis. Downtown is unsafe and unpredictable. Like an American city.

MR WESTMAN. You can only blame the deficit and the . . .

CHAT. . . . and the lack of the aggressive entrepreneurial spirit!

DECOSTA. Well, what do you expect? All the aggression is after hours, in the dark. There is no business that is safe, these days.

BOSE. By the way, how are things, Paul?. . . That neighbourhood is getting a bit rough, eh . . . And with Jack gone . . .

DECOSTA. I'm managing somehow . . . but Jack was a special guy. He kept the place alive.

BOSE. I know. Any clues . . . did the MUC come up with something . . . I heard . . .

DECOSTA (*quick*). What did you hear?

BOSE. Just that Jack had a clean record, and it may have been a case of mistaken identity. Did you hear anything?

DECOSTA. I have not heard anything. It was very unfortunate. Five years with me. Managed everything by himself. I did not worry about anything. Now there is an emptiness . . . also a drop in the business . . . I am not a barman . . . He was . . . The bar was known for him.

CHAT. He was quite a character, from what I've heard, eh? Knew something about everybody . . . First name basis . . . Maybe you should change the name of the bar . . .

BOSE. Change the name! Everybody knows everybody, out there. Changing names won't make a difference.

CHAT. Oh, from a business point of view, I would do it . . .

MRS CHAT. I heard it was a very brutal ending. There is some speculation that the murder weapon had a hook or an angle at the end . . . and it rips the guts out with it . . . (*music*).

CHAT. Check on you!

BOSE (*he is stunned by the move, apparently*). Where did you read about that?

MRS CHAT. Anita. You know, the girl who goes to Concordia. She mentioned it to me. I believe she is quite a fan of yours. They are supposed to come tonight. (*Bose is staring down at the board.*)

WEST. Awful, you know. I'm amazed at the number of unsolved murders in Montreal. The numbers seem to be growing.

DECOSTA. Have there been any other murders in this region?

CHAT. Oh! Quite a few, actually. And I think there is a link. I'm not suggesting that Jack had anything to do with it. But rumours are that the drug scene is moving into that part of town. You know, the smart stuff. Pricey.

DECOSTA. Jack was clean. Whoever killed him, made a big mistake or knew something, that only Jack knew.

CHAT. Ah! Look who's here.

Gene and Anita enter. DeCosta looks a bit disturbed, but conceals it by going to the waiter and getting a drink. Chatterjee introduces Jim Westman. Everybody wishes everybody and shakes hands.

DECOSTA (*to Mrs Chat*). I shall be leaving soon.

MRS CHAT. Oh! Come on, it's just nine. What's the matter with you? Cheer up. I will fix you a stiff one. Rusty nail? Yes?

DECOSTA. No, thank you. I have some new people at the bar. Students . . . and they don't know all the ropes. Plus the regulars, Jack's friends. I must make sure they do not quit coming.

MRS CHAT. I'm so sorry. Darling! Paul has to leave.

CHAT (*gets up*). Listen, Paul. (*Draws him aside and they talk softly.*) OK?

DECOSTA. Sure, I understand. OK. Bye, everybody.

GENE. Hey, Mr DeCosta, I need to see you sometime . . . (*He follows him out for a while . . . comes back a little later, and starts chatting with Chatterjee and Westman.*)

ANITA. Prof. Bose, I was wondering . . .

BOSE. Oh, hullo . . . I heard you were working . . .

ANITA. On the Sulpician Escarpment . . .

BOSE. Fascinating, is it not . . .?

ANITA. . . . Absolutely . . . but there are so many angles to the whole region that it is not really properly documented . . . I mean nobody seems to have bothered to write anything down . . . even the church records are obscure.

BOSE. Well, that's where you have to sort of resort to the oral tradition . . . you have to talk to the long-time residents, listen to the local folk music, some of the theatre, read up some of the legal text.

ANITA. You mean hang out at the local bar scene . . .

BOSE. Yes, yes! That plus the CP rail files.

ANITA. There is so much storytelling in the local bars. Gossip galore!

BOSE. The gossip in the bars is really a way of keeping the story alive. The word gossip is a bit demeaning, here. There is a lot of unwritten oral tradition, especially in the taverns. Especially in the Point region . . .

ANITA. Yeah, the Point, the Point, the Point. Ever since I came to Montreal, two years ago, everybody has to make a point about the Point! Don't people ever get tired about writing about the struggling working class of the Point, and their daily battles against the folks living up on the hill! Seems like everybody's made a killing, writing about the Point. What's the real score?

BOSE. Well, there was a time when there were a lot of grassroots community groups doing work there. Everytime you turned on a CBC radio show—there was somebody berating the world for neglecting the region . . . and it's true . . . solid people, with a long history battling the system, with a lot of street savvy. But it's all slowly dying out . . .

ANITA. Is it true . . . you know I was reading, the other day, that the fault line that runs along the edge of the city . . . was really a mound built by the Mohawks, several centuries ago . . . and at the Museum I found out that the ridge was there since prehistoric times . . . Which is true?

BOSE. The ridge provides a natural barrier . . . but was never built by the Mohawks . . . it's a pure fault line, from a centuries-old shift . . .

MRS CHAT (*butting in*). Well, isn't that interesting . . . Can I get you something to drink, dear?

ANITA. I'm fine, thank you. And the word is that . . . Gene! Prof. Bose knows quite a bit about the Escarpment.

GENE (*comes over*). Oh yeah. Jack told me, he was the top gun on the ridge . . . (*laughs*) . . . So what's the score, Prof. Bose . . . have you heard the latest controversy? The folks in the taverns say . . . there is an angle to the ridge which is in dispute.

BOSE. I am not aware of such a controversy . . . !

GENE. Oh! Yes! In fact, there's been columns in the paper . . . with city mappers saying that they've measured the incline . . . and it's fifteen degrees from the top . . . down . . . meanwhile at the taverns they sing songs about the seventy-five degree slope uphill . . . a real battle is on, what do you say?

BOSE. I think it is a tempest in a teapot . . . How does it matter . . . ? Doesn't city hall have anything else to discuss?

MRS CHAT. But is it not obvious? I mean from high school geometry, if the angle is seventy-five degrees from the bottom . . .

ANITA. The point is that the people at the bottom of the ridge feel that their view is not being considered . . . If you look at the city from the bottom it's a seventy-five degree slope up . . .

GENE. So which is it, Prof.? Maybe I can have a snapshot of you on the ridge pondering over the angle . . . We could do a piece in the westend section . . .

ANITA. Oh! Gene!

BOSE. Let me get a drink . . . I will join you in a second . . .

CHAT. Ah, I see you have some admirers, Bose!

Anita and Gene start talking to each other softly. Bose goes over to Chatterjee. Mrs Chatterjee is talking with Westman. Bose and Chatterjee start talking rather animatedly. A sound track develops . . like a deep cello . . . which drowns out everybody, but each group is seen conferring intently. The waiter comes by with a smile on his face, pushing a trolley. He goes from one group to another to the accompaniment of the music. He finally reaches Chatterjee. He opens the lid to the tray and Chatterjee deftly picks up a rather large curved knife, with which he starts cutting into a slice of ham . . . the lights close in and then fade out.

GENE (*moving a piece, and looking at Anita*). Hey, there is a mate here!

Chatterjee smiles as he cuts into the ham. Bose ponders with a drink in his hand.

Scene 8

Anita is seen fast asleep on the same table that Gene was working on. It is a dream sequence. Above, on a riser or a scaffold, one man, barebodied, is seen going through motions of tai-chi silhouetted against a dense red smoke lit background. The sound track is very industrial and it ends with gunfire shots taking over and it gets louder and louder, until the man seems like he is shot and collapses. Like an apparition, set twenty years ago. The young man appears upstage centre. He has a blood patch on his shirt. Once more the faint sound of a rail car going by in the distance.

YOUNG MAN. Years later people are gonna tell you that I was really a wagon breaker. Somebody who lived off the hot merchandise ripped from the railway wagons. Or maybe a pimp. It does not matter. The point is, that it does not even matter whether I did what I did, out of a belief in certain ideals. There are no ideals that can stand the test of time . . . no truism is permanent. In fact, what I did was very simple. In the slum behind the railway lines, where nobody from my parents' neighbourhood would dare to go, or cross the ridge . . . where a bunch of thugs ran the slum with the cops to protect them . . . I got the young kids together. Tell them not to pay the thugs . . . Stop greeting them. No confrontation. Just cold shoulder and stalling. That's it. This goes on for a while. Until the cops get restless. No pay coming their way, either! So one day, the thugs rough up somebody and the cops pretend they don't see. So next day, you get a cop in a dark alley. Everybody helps. You know. And then we clobber the shit out of him. Tie him to a cart and deposit him in front of the chief thug's headquarters. All hell breaks loose. The cops clear out. You get more people interested and you start organizing one alley after another. Sounds simple, right? Yeah! But it does not work, my friend. It does not work in the long run . . . Now I tell you . . . Most people are ready to fight for what they believe in. Or, at least give it an honest first try. If that succeeds, well you got a battle in your hands, and there is no walking away. And let me tell you something else . . . most people in the world believe in a good fight. The problem is that during a lull in the fight, they have to get back to the mundane shit . . . feed the kids, worry about some savings, pay off some debt . . . it's the human angle, my friend. The living dilemma. The battle to survive.

And that keeps coming back at you. Gnawing away at your tenacity. Chewing away at your zeal to fight and sapping it dull. The battle to live out life is a burden, my friend. (*Sound track*) Shit, if only there was somebody out there to subsidize a good fight for change! There's no corporate donation for subversive activity, huh? But the Company is always there, my friend. Lurking in the shadows, protecting the helicopters in the skies. You know the Company? No? There would be no problem, my mother would be a happy woman . . . (*He smiles. Silence.*) But don't let your guard down, like I did. Don't let them creep up on ya! It hurts, my friend! It's a sharp wound, when it goes into your guts and tears it out. One moment, like a bout with eternity. Cold steel, plunging through your flesh, and sawing through your bones and then the deadly retraction. Like your whole inside is wrenched away from you. It's the steep angle of the blade, my friend, the dividing line. The steep angle always between life and death . . . (*Lights off on young man. Sound track of the flutter of wings. Lights on Anita. She wakes up, very restless. She calls out to Gene several times . . .*)

Scene 9

Night. Gene at a pay phone, on a street corner. Focused street light, in a sharp zone. Repeatedly looks at his watch. Finally, dials a number while reading it from a scrap of paper.

GENE. Hullo! Hi! this is Gene Burris . . . There was a message on my machine . . .Yes . . . that's right . . . regarding what? . . . Yes, I do . . . Yes, I am very much interested . . . but I'd like to know . . . sorry? . . .Yes . . . but . . . sir, what is your name . . . sorry? . . . it is important . . . I kept . . .Yes, but you asked me to use this pay phone . . . and I did . . . you asked me to call at 8.05 on the dot and I did . . . I have not violated . . . so you should keep your end of the deal . . . Yes, there was a deal in the works, the moment you left a message . . . (*Silence for a while*) I shall. Yes. Yes, no there is no one else with me. Yes, I understand. I shall wait. (*Puts the phone down. He is looking at one direction, staring out. The stage is pitch dark, elsewhere. It is a cold night. He paces in a tight circle. Looks at his watch. Then, as if he has seen something, he squints his eye and looks to one side of the stage. A person, waiting in the dark, lights a cigarette. The man is dressed exactly like the person, who has been seen walking away after each murder.The man starts walking slowly towards Gene.*)

MAN. Don't turn around and raise your hands!

GENE. What?

Man frisks him quickly.

MAN. No tapes, eh?

GENE. No tapes.

Man walks away slowly.

CHAT (*takes his hat off to reveal his identity*). Listen, Mr Sherlock Holmes.

GENE. Mr Chatterjee! I swear . . .

CHAT. Twenty years ago, just like you, I was looking for a lead, also. (*Chatterjee walks around Gene in half circles.*)

GENE. . . . I could never have recognized your voice.

CHAT. Different kind of lead, though. And I never worked for anybody. Never wanted to. Least of all, as a paperboy! Hah! I scavenged the world for leads, for connections. Connections, my friend. Connections to engage in enterprise. That's what—

GENE. Mr Chatterjee, I have never doubted . . .

CHAT. Don't interrupt me, just listen to me very carefully. I don't have too much time for all this. I sense that you are digging deep into the Jack Simard case.

GENE. As a matter of fact . . .

CHAT. Before you go off on the wrong track, I thought I would let you know some salient facts about this case. In this part of the world, investigations often go off on a tangent. Before we try to find out who killed Jack Simard, we must know, who was Jack Simard? And, why would I, Ace Chatterjee, who has no use for this type of shit, no reason to meet a stringer like you in a dark alley . . . After all I know, a journalist is a journalist. If you open your mouth to one of them, just for a few minutes, he has already written a serial which will run for three days. Right?

GENE. You asked me not to interrupt.

CHAT. Yes, I did. But something in me told me that you are a stuck-up sonofabitch who will not take the easy road, with a cheap shot at a crime beat story. That you will investigate, before you blab!

GENE. Ah! I take it as a compliment, from a man with your connections, sir!

CHAT. My connections tell me Jack Simard, was not Jack Simard. He was not even a Quebecer.

GENE. What?

CHAT. He was an American. An important American.

GENE. Jack was a Yank?

CHAT. In 1965, he was in the South East Asia operations of the Company.

GENE. The Company! You mean . . .

CHAT. When I say the Company, I don't mean the United Fruit Company, comprendo, amigo? Although it could very well be so. I mean the venerable Central Intelligence Agency.

GENE. You knew him? In India?

CHAT. No! I did not. But I found out later. From somebody else. Only when I came to Montreal.

GENE. DeCosta?

CHAT. Jack was in Vietnam. Spoke French fluently. Worked out of Bangkok. Was with the Special Forces, assigned to McNamara. Ever heard his name, kid?

GENE. Wasn't he . . .

CHAT. Never mind. The fact of the matter is that in 1967 he was brought into Calcutta. Soft duty, as they would call it. Technology officer! In the US Consulate. But his main job was liaison . . . which is Company slang for keeping tabs on all local insurgencies, surrounding the main arena of war, from Burma and Thailand to Bengal and Nepal. By infiltrating the local police force.

GENE. DeCosta was a cop?

CHAT. Nope, but again you are interrupting me!

GENE. Did Jack know DeCosta then?

CHAT. Maybe, maybe not. But again you are getting interested in the tangent. In the stuff that distracts. Try to enter the circle, not slip and slide on its circumference! What is important . . . and you have not bothered to ask me, until now . . . is . . . why did Jack Simard end up in Montreal?

GENE. I was just . . .

CHAT. Going to ask me? Right. Listen, Jack Simard aka Jason Sinclair, became a CO in the early seventies, when Nixon was bombing the hell out of Cambodia and denying it, just like we know that old rat . . .

GENE. CO? Did you say CO?

CHAT. Ah yes! CO—Conscientious Objector. Jack couldn't take it any more. The duplicity of US policy. Especially in Asia. But it was too late. You can't become a CO when you work for the Company. Not like the college kids could . . .

GENE. . . . or like Muhammad Ali . . .

CHAT. Yes Cassius Clay, was his name. Except, unlike Clay, Jack boxed in the shadows, in the dark, without world titles. You know what I mean. So he would not suffer from being a celebrity. So Jack jumped Uncle Sam . . . disappeared . . .

GENE. To Montreal! Wow! But wait a minute. So what's that have to do with DeCosta?

CHAT. Did I say it had to? And that's what I wanted to make sure you knew. The tangent you shouldn't go off on. DeCosta is somebody I've gotten to like. He means no harm to no one. He should be left alone.

GENE. Are you suggesting, Mr Chatterjee, that I lay off . . .

CHAT. No such thing. Just making sure you don't go off on a tangent. In fact, I'm telling you to go on, dig deeper. Remember what you said at the party. DeCosta and Jack . . . like they . . .

GENE. Got each other in their . . . grips.

CHAT. Right! They had become friends. Close friends, over the years. But the friendship was dangerous. Paul had come to know Jack's secret . . .

GENE. But Paul had a skeleton too . . .! So they covered for each other!

CHAT. And Paul's secret, my dear fellow, is not cloak and dagger stuff . . .

GENE. What is it?

CHAT. Ask Paul!

GENE. Mr DeCosta! He ain't gonna talk shit to me, man! The man splits when he sees me, like he's seen a ghost.

CHAT. Try again! He's ready. He needs to talk. And keep me out of all this . . . for ever. I have nothing to do with all this. I really couldn't care less. Just thought I'd let you know. Because Paul is nervous. But he wants to talk. I wouldn't talk to you if he didn't want me to. It seems he's got some notions—

GENE. Wait a minute . . .

CHAT. . . . Before something big happens. He wants to get over his little problem. Listen, I'm off. (*Pulls out a cellular phone from inside his jacket, punches in a number, starts walking away, briskly, into the dark, while talking. Gene looks at him. Car start sound and fade away.*)

GENE (*talks to himself*). Jack worked for the Company. Turned CO and peeled cover to start off again in Montreal. DeCosta knew all about it, from Calcutta. DeCosta had something to hide. Jack knew about it. Jack gets taken out twenty years later in Montreal. DeCosta's nervous. Wants to talk to me. And Mr. Ace Chatterbox pulls a Bogart on me at a secret rendezvous, 'cause he likes DaCosta! Fuck, am I being setup or am I being setup? What the fuck is going on . . . (*rushes over to the phone booth . . . punches in numbers*).

Scene 10

In Gene's room. Anita and Prof. Bose walk in together. Looks like they have been together for a while. Anita goes over to the side, hangs up his jacket and hers. Bose looks around.

BOSE. This is a comfortable place.

ANITA. Yes, it is. Prof. Bose, can I get you something to drink?

BOSE. Sure.

ANITA. What would you like?

BOSE. Oh! It does not matter. If you have some rye, that's fine. Yes.

ANITA. Well! Gene likes rye too! How 'bout that? (*She fixes two drinks and brings them back. Both sit down on chairs near the table with the laptop.*)

BOSE. Is Gene out on assignment?

ANITA. Oh no! He is around somewhere.

BOSE. There was something I wanted to ask you, before we were so rudely interrupted by that fellow at the bar . . .

ANITA. Right! The exact angle of the slope . . . the Escarpment.

BOSE. Well, . . . the angle of the Escarpment! Yes, I find that such a ridiculously . . .

ANITA. Peripheral issue?

BOSE. Well! I mean, the entire faculty seems to be engulfed in it. Everywhere they are discussing it.

ANITA. A controversy seems to be brewing over it . . . but it seems it's a part of the folklore too, and it cannot really be suppressed. The angle of the slope!

BOSE. What is important is the gentrification that has occurred and the severe economic downturn of the entire area below the ridge . . . (*agitated*). The issue is not the angle. The issue is the fact of the difference in the two levels. Between the hill and the flats down below. Anyway, how does it bloody matter, if the angle is sevnty-five degrees from the top . . .

ANITA. . . . or fifteen degrees from the bottom of the slope! . . . (*Both stare at each other in a searching manner. He swigs his drink down and pours himself another.*) Anyway, I have decided to steer clear of the whole issue by titling my thesis 'The Sulpician Escarpment: The Slope that Divides.' That way, we are clear of the controversy . . . no mention of angles. (*They both laugh. Bose gets up to walk around with his drink and wanders over to Gene's desk, from behind. Anita is watching him, but reading mail, quickly.*)

BOSE. I wanted to ask you . . . I heard you mention at the Chatterjees' that Jack Simard was stabbed with a . . . is that right?

ANITA (*whips around*). Yes, rather brutally. Didn't you know? From the back. It was . . .

BOSE. From the back! Who told you that?

ANITA. The people at the bar.

BOSE. People at the bar! But nobody told me that. Just when you think you've found a place of . . . very unfortunate, he was such a . . . Who could do that to Jack? (*Bose sits down at Gene's desk and stares into the papers. Anita gets up and stares straight out, while she talks. Sound track. In this episode, as Anita builds up her story, Bose seems to get more and more unsettled.*)

ANITA. Very interesting character, Jack! I had a chance to talk to him, just recently. For quite a while! (*Walks around.*) He told me he was scared for his life . . . Could not trust the shadows around him. Old shadows that were growing larger and larger, to haunt him, every night as he stalked through the streets. Like he had a dark past himself. He really opened up with me. Seems like, he's known you for a long time . . .

BOSE (*turns around*). Who? Me? Ah, yes! I've known him . . .

ANITA. I mean, didn't you know him before you came to Canada? (*Bose has a quick swig.*)

BOSE. Not really . . . Actually, I am quite disturbed by his death. Now you are telling me it was so brutal!

ANITA. He was stabbed with a very sharp weapon. The weapon had an angle to it.

BOSE. But the police report said he was shot . . .

ANITA. Do you believe everything the police say? Do you? The assailant was known to Jack. Like a friend. (*Bose winces and gets up.*) From a past, long time ago. Not the regular hit man type. Not the type who'd lurk around in dark alleys. Respectable type. According to the Squad investigating the murder. Jack was apparently stabbed first in the back . . .

BOSE. But I distinctly remember a police report saying he was shot . . .

ANITA. . . . then as he turned to fall . . . he must have recognized his assailant.

BOSE. How could you?. . .You were not . . .

ANITA. Somebody he knew. Maybe from a long time back. Maybe

a person he had trusted in. Maybe somebody who shared a common past. The sense of betrayal in Jack's eyes was obvious.

BOSE. How do you know all this? (*Anita ignores him.*)

ANITA. As Jack fell on his back, the assailant lunged into him, a deep jab, only once, just below the solar plexus. The knife has a edge to it, Professor Bose, as it goes in.

BOSE. Please . . .

ANITA. Another edge as it comes out.

BOSE. That knife, nobody here . . .

ANITA. And as the knife was withdrawn, it cut his guts out in coils. (*Bose sits down, as in a collapse.*) It is a sharp wound, when it tears into your guts and rips it out. One moment, like a bout with eternity. Cold steel plunging through your flesh, and sawing through your bones and then the deadly retraction . . .

BOSE. Please stop, Anita!

ANITA. Like your whole inside is wrenched away from you . . . the blade, it is the angle of the blade that does the job . . . (*Behind a scrim the bartender is heard laughing gently . . . and the young man is seen standing with the bloodied shirt, tottering as if like a silhouette, near him.*)

BOSE (*softly*). No! Stop! Stop this drama, Anita! Jack was shot! Stop it! Nobody here has such a knife!

ANITA (*coming towards him*). Why, Professor Bose! Is it the steep angle of the blade . . . or is it the two edges? Is that the same controversy about the Escarpment, the dividing line . . . Only you know about it?

BOSE. Jack was not stabbed!

ANITA. Oh! And you know? With such confidence?

BOSE. Yes! I do! Let's bring some sanity into this whole situation . . . I thought you had invited me over to discuss your thesis . . . and where is Gene?

ANITA. Gene will be here shortly. Professor Bose, there is an uncanny association, continents apart. The slope and the angle. Controversy and folklore. People on top say one thing, people down below knock it down. And twenty years later! The same blade!

BOSE. I don't know what you are talking about! I have to go.

(Bose has turned his back to the audience and has put on his jacket . . . suddenly his shoes sound like the shoes of the assailant in the first scene.)

ANITA. The steep angle between life and death.

BOSE. Why are you telling me all this?

ANITA. You know why I'm telling you all this!

BOSE. No! I don't! I cannot stand this gory—

ANITA. Oh, yes! You can . . . You could twenty years ago . . .

BOSE. What? What are you taking about? Look, this is very unpleasant . . .What are you trying to do? (*Bose starts to walk away.*)

ANITA. Don't walk away, Professor Bose!

BOSE. I have to go . . . Jack . . . was a close friend.

ANITA. Yes, close enough . . . you owed him one . . ., he got you out of a mess, he let you fly, but don't walk away! You did that once before!

BOSE. I don't know what you are talking about! This is getting a bit out of hand. I am getting late!

ANITA. Late? Late for what, Professor Bose? It took me twenty years to find my brother's killer . . . it is still not late . . . you are not walking away this time, you bastard. . .

BOSE. What!

Bose whips around and looks at her, with murderous eyes, completely transformed. He moves towards her. Gene jumps out from behind a platform and grabs Bose from the back. Bose swings free, ferociously, whips out a knife, and is about to stab Gene.

ANITA. Don't even think about it.

She has a revolver in her grip. She cocks it. Bose slowly turns to look at Anita. Then his looks change. Slowly there is resignation in his eyes. He stares at Anita. Anita takes the knife from him and drops it to the ground. There is a sound track of a bird fluttering till it is heard louder and louder until it comes crashing to the ground. Bose is staring at the knife, stuck on the floor. As lights dim very slowly, Bose mutters away. Only Bose and the knife are under a spot of light.

BOSE. I did not kill Jack. I could never do it to him. I could never. He was my friend. He brought me here. Why would I kill him? This is a big mistake, I did not kill him! I did not kill Jack. I know he was shot. You made it all up. This is a big lie! This is a big lie! You tricked me! You tricked me, you bitch! You tricked me. Wait a minute! You killed . . .

A gunfire sound is heard. Bose collapses to the ground. A warm brassy sound track plays the original theme tune. Sound track overlaps with All India Radio announcement faint in the background . . . to the effect that well-known history professor at Montreal's McGill University and former resident of Calcutta and . . . the assailant is a student of Indian origin who has disappeared . . .

Appendix

'What politicized me was the power of performance'

An interview with Rana Bose by Uma Parameswaran

Rana is an intellectual dissenter. All his plays highlight the theme of protest, not specific injustices or individual incidents of suffering so much as the systemic shortcomings that give rise to and perpetuate an unjust society. In *Baba Jacques*, for instance, he speaks of the systemic ghettoization of the Indo-Canadian community, that is both self-imposed, and government-imposed by the policy of multiculturalism. *Five or Six Characters* is a fast-paced lampooning of what he calls 'tribalism', and he has the action taking place on the highway between Montreal and Toronto, with half a dozen characters representing various tribes. While the Canadian audience would readily identify the tribe of hockey jocks and the loaded political satire, the Indian reader would also see immediate relevance in the fundamentalist who is carrying a brick to build a church in Toronto and in the flatulent literary-criticism jargon of the academic, both of whom are among the passengers in the bus that crashes into the tunnel of Time Zero.

As though the dialogues are not abstruse enough, Rana uses stage effects that are kaleidoscopic. Small wonder that his plays do not fly in a country where racial minorities are not expected to be sophisticated or intellectual when writing about their life in Canada.

This interview was conducted in his house in Montreal on 24 March 1996. What follows is an excerpt from that interview.

Uma: I have written about your plays and about Montreal Serai in various places such as the *Toronto South Asian Review, Canadian Theatre Review* and in *Contemporary Issues in Canadian Drama*. Also, the literary qualities and the political thrusts of your plays can be drawn out of your texts if one is willing to put in some critical effort and do one's homework about the political realities around us in Canada. So today I would like to get some background information that only you can give. Tell us something about the early influences in your life that have shaped your theatrical imagination.

Rana: When you phoned me two days ago about the questions you had in mind for today's meeting, it set me thinking for the first time about some aspects of my work that I had never consciously given thought to before.

My interest in theatre—I think it started with my father taking me in the late fifties and early sixties to see Utpal Dutt's Little Theatre Group in Calcutta at the Minerva Theatre, and what really overwhelmed me about Utpal Dutt's group was the power of their acting and their visual attack on the senses. Even as a child I was overwhelmed by the power of their theatre. It was only later that I came to know about Utpal Dutt's political beliefs. Over the years I have come to have a cynical disregard for unsubtle attempts at using the stage as a pulpit. What came through to me was that Utpal Dutt, like Rod Steiger, or Marlon Brando in *A Streetcar Named Desire,* had a kind of personality, handsome, with a broad forehead . . . an extremely powerful presence.

At the same time, there was something else. Utpal Dutt had a stage craftsman, Tapas Sen; Tapas Sen was an incredible character; even in those days, when facilities were rather primitive compared to what can be done now, he created this magnificent spectacle on stage; I went to see his *Kallol,* about the Naval Mutiny, and he had erected the whole bow of a ship on the stage, and was firing cannon balls straight into the audience; the deck of the ship was on the main aisle, and you could see trapdoors popping open and ratings jumping out and the rebel navy men rushing forward. It was so powerful. . . and then there was *Neecher Mahal,* the Bengali version of *Lower Depths.* . . and *Nil Darpan,* on the Indigo Revolt, another classic. I still remember the great line from that play. When the English forced our people to cultivate blue dye for export, instead of cultivating rice and wheat, the peasants rose in revolt and the war cry was, 'This hand won't sow blue dye any more!' I was five years old then, but I can hear it even now.

The power of the theatre got under my skin as politics; all

these were political plays using theatre but it was the theatre part that got me going about politics, the other way around you know, even though there was a long tradition in my family of left-wing association. At the same time, there was this cultural thing, I don't mean poetry, dance etc., but a personal culture, meaning an affiliation with one's behaviour, values, an open association with a way of life that is multi-dimensional, a blend, a mix of many temperaments—'foreign' and 'domestic'.

I grew up in a neighbourhood called Elliot Road in Calcutta. By conditioning, I didn't grow up as an urban Bengali boy; I grew up in an Anglo-Indian milieu.

Uma: Why was this? You said in an earlier conversation that your family were left-wing; did that have something to do with where you lived?

Rana: My parents were working professionals. They had travelled abroad, and studied abroad, and my father was working in down-town central Calcutta and we always lived in that part, before my birth in Creek Row and Dharamtola Street, and then Elliot Road, and these were all non-Bengali, non-Hindu areas—they were Anglo-Indian, Christian and Muslim neighbourhoods; around the Park Street area, not in the posh areas like Camac Street and Hungerford Street where many mill managers lived.

My father Amiya Kumar Bose, was a doctor, a heart specialist; besides being a top-notch cardiologist, he was very much a social activist; for instance, the Students' Health Home in Calcutta was founded by him; in our house. The People's Relief Committee, which gave help in times of floods and other disasters, was founded by him. He was the founder, or one of several in a group, and now those places are huge—Students' Health Home now has a six-storey hospital—but all of them started in a house, our house; my father was into frontline grassroots activism, which, of course, didn't go well with his professional milieu. But he was also President of the Indian Science Congress at the Madras session . . . which was the first time I visited Madras.

My mother was a professional statistician, she was not into politics, she kept out of it because she was a government bureau-crat; but I have a sneaking suspicion that she always voted left, and never told anyone about it. Anyway, I went to St. Xavier's

School, which was a very anglicized environment; so my cultural upbringing was cross-bred, and I didn't go for Rabindra Sangeet. I am not defensive when I say this; I don't think I missed a lot. But at the same time, my father was a doctor for Tagore, and so we were connected to the Tagore family. Despite that, my cultural needs were already embedded somewhat differently. I had a hungry need for doing all kinds of things, and was not interested in being tied to any one kind of culture. I had to have it all, under the belt.

Theatre caught my interest, especially Tapas Sen's lighting . . . when I do my theatre here in Montreal today, I realized, in the last couple of days since you asked me to think of early influences, that the origins of my techno theatre, my nineties theatre, using a lot of techniques, a lot of effects, is actually rooted in Tapas Sen's enormous stagecraft. Those were the fifties, primitive; can you imagine, there was nothing, no motorized strobes, couldn't patch panels together, no computerization, not like now when we have so many dimmers—in an average auditorium today we have fifteen, twenty dimmers, and of course now you have them, all the fancy stuff, in Calcutta too, and yet that man achieved such dramatic effects with next to nothing. Now, in the nineties, you see Carbon-14 and La La La and Human Steps and Edouard Locke and their avant-garde performance. I am not saying one or the other influenced me. But I am saying that all that came together in my poor man's theatre; it will always be a poor man's theatre because I am convinced that I will never get funding. We don't have the ability; when I say that, I don't mean theatrical ability but the political savvy to get funded, I don't know how to lick the right butts; it takes that; I am not demeaning it, but anyway, going back to my roots, there were these experiences of going with my father, and these epic performances, *Kallol* and *Manusher Adhikarey,* which is much later . . . and Tapas Sen's tremendous stagecraft made me politicized much more than the actual politics did; mind you, my family had a lot of left-wing associations, with people coming and going through our house; when the Communist Party was banned, people came to our house for shelter, and so I'd meet all kinds of personalities, I could rattle off names, but that's not what politicized me; what politicized me was the power of performance. So there I was, not actually into theatre but subliminally affected by the visual attack that theatre gave to the senses; just imagine, you see a flaming jeep on stage and you see a policeman roughing up somebody . . . it makes a permanent mark on you. We didn't have television then. There was no Rodney King being roughed up by police on TV.

So I was still not in theatre as such, though I had this subliminal persuasion. Then we come to the late sixties and seventies, and I get politically involved in the student movement and a lot of things happen on campus . . .

And then, the next phase in theatre involvement took a different turn. While one wanted to be naturally a leftist, and be affiliated with progressive and democratic causes, there was a big cultural vacuum in the movement in terms of political culture; not in terms of activities, because there was a lot of singing and dancing and composing and theatre going on, but within the organization, there was a culture of feudalism. It was often quite feudal. No matter how industrialized a society is, feudalism thrives. For me, feudalism is a power you wield over people; it is an extra-political power, an undemocratic kind of exertion on everybody. Theatre is an outlet; it is liberatory, it lets you do what the *dadas* and gurus won't let you do; once you are into theatre, you go wild. Then there is that romantic imagery, all over the world revolt is happening, free speech movement, Sorbonne, Berkeley, Berlin, Prague. I read the poetry of the beat generation—Ginsberg, Kerouac, Burroughs . . . these expressions may sound clichéd but it appealed to me that words, rhythms—call them bohemian if you will—on-the-road literature, appealed to me, in terms of visual and oral attack; jazz poetry that I use today in readings of my poetry in Montreal, all have roots in a kind of social curiosity, in my upbringing, my father taking me to see theatre . . . he would never preach, just say 'look at this, read this, what do you think of this' . . . all this gelled together, when in the sixties and seventies I got involved . . . I realized that all organizations, even the most radical ones, could be radical but were internally, culturally, living within the realm of society, which was semi-feudal; there was no escape from it.

Some of the things that happened in the Naxalite movement had to do with the feudal culture within the organization; very rigid codified guilt-tripping, class-consciousness in reverse. This is a lower-middle-class thing . . . An enormous glorification of physical suffering; in the olden days it was said that if you didn't have tuberculosis, you were not a good communist, and if you were not dying of hunger, you couldn't be a good party activist, but I thought it was more important to do something, regardless of background and daily meals. There was all this romanticist energy at work. Che [Guevara] was not dead, even though in the Maoist movement he was considered totally incorrect . . . On the one hand, there was the genuine affiliation with the working poor, but at the same time, there was a need to do things that were powerful; all that romantic energy . . . the storming of the Bastille was like political theatre, like taking the cobblestones apart, bombarding the headquarters, raising flags!

Then, when I started doing theatre in college, well, I was only marginally involved, mainly because all the theatre was in Bengali and my knowledge of Bengali was not enough; in fact I learnt Bengali only after I left home and went underground; so I hung around like a groupie, helping with stage . . . like when, on the street, we needed a lot of workers, literally physically cordoning off the street stage from violent interruptions by holding hands around it, and at this time theatre became an increasingly dangerous occupation. So here was Dutt and Badal Sircar and Rudraprasad [Sengupta] and all the old radicals, and the Minerva Theatre, and then there was the open theatre, Muktangan, that was increasingly coming under attack under Mrs Gandhi's rule; the police would come and open fire. In fact one of the most painful incidents in my life was the killing of Prabir [Dutta], a friend, when he was acting, while he was on stage, not a stage so much as the street, of course, but it was like Hyde Park in those days, and he was bludgeoned to death in cold blood by a policeman.

It was at this time that it struck me, that my father, who was the founder of APDR (the Association for the Protection of Democratic Rights) was opening my eyes to the basic cultural need for democracy. It was the beginnings of the civil liberties movement; even we, who were in the left, had no idea of civil liberties, we thought of it as a wimpy thing, to talk of civil liberties, while the armed struggle was going on in Vietnam etc. but later on I realized that these were the people who were the real bourgeois democrats of our country, my father and his generation, who studied in England in the twenties and thirties, who were trying to introduce the concept of personal liberties and individual rights, that the concepts had to be ingrained. Only Bengali theatre taught me about civil liberties.

Even up to this point, I had been only marginally involved in theatre. I had not done theatre. I had been going outside Calcutta to faraway places, like Khurda, which had a phenomenal theatre movement. It was street theatre and guerrilla theatre, and then came the repression. I ended up in jail for quite a long time; I got busted for my student activism. Indira Gandhi had jailed over 30,000 in one shot.

Uma: Was this for theatre activities?

Rana: No, it was for my student involvement; they amassed a lot of charges against me; at one time, they had something like thirty charges against me. That was typical of the times. The ambassador to the United States now, Siddhartha [Shankar] Ray, was the chief minister.

They withdrew all the charges and then detained me on the Preventive Detention Act. Those were very gruesome, very politically educating times, and then I literally had to exile myself. I had dropped out of school for five years . . . and after I got out of jail, there was no place for me; no college would re-admit me. The whole movement had dissipated; I always suffered from ideals of cultural liberation, I think I really believed we could do something; you know what Emma Goldman has said: 'If I can't dance, I don't want to be part of your revolution'; even though I didn't know the statement then, I knew it was the way I felt. But the liberation didn't happen. I left India at the time virtually as an exile, and I reluctantly started working very hard at an engineering degree and completed it in record time—two and a half years.

At that time, when I was on campus, the Vietnam war was coming to an end and Watergate was happening, and of course I got involved. That's when I came to know about the technology of theatre and started writing poetry, it was probably quite effete. My black roommate got me into jazz poetry and theatre and then I saw the San Francisco Mime Troupe, and the Vermont Bread and Butter Theatre, and all this revived in me the sense of liberatory theatre but it was not the Brechtian theatre, *The Good Woman of Szechuan* and all that kind which had impressed me in Calcutta, but this was mask drama and poster drama—and all that was going on in the USA at the time. I took theatre courses—at Washington University in St. Louis—and I learnt the basics of stage production; I did some stage lighting and designing for a band—Gerry Mulligan's—he was a saxophonist—as part of a course. It made me understand what Tapas Sen was doing fifteen years earlier with the crudest possible devices. Then came the Emergency and I came to Montreal and started writing plays. It was very difficult at first, didactic, poster drama straight out of the seventies. But now it is different. There is this enormous influence of Brecht, to entertain and educate through song and dance, the concept of epic theatre . . . and then there is the influence of jazz and my tremendous affinity for music, movement and imagery. I am also thus propelled towards multi-media theatre and this is where Carbon-14 and others come in.

And now what has happened is that living in Canada and Quebec and Montreal, my world has gelled to a Montrealais environment. And all those years of India, politics, Utpal Dutt, Sircar, my father, the great melancholy I feel for my father's absence in my life even now, though he's been gone for twenty-one years, my stay in the US, all is distilled into Montreal, here in 1996, referendum, tribal politics worldwide. At the same time, I am an engineer, senior executive in a very large Canadian company, and that has brought in a technological bent, a desire for precision, a multi-dimensional cultural edge—to perform on the borderlines and expand the borders. Everything that is happening around us has made me wary of borders. Borders will always exist, but I believe in extending borders, extending and bringing them to the centre, of blending.

Uma: You seem to have your own definition of 'blending' that is not used in the usual sense of mixing.

Rana: Blending is for me a kind of political assertion that is inclusive. I feel that I can just as well define the terms of inclusion rather than demand to be included. We have to go beyond making demands to be included. We have to be taking the lead; saying, 'Want to join? Come on.' We should lay the ground rules for inclusion. That way we won't have to worry about being excluded.

Everything we do is political; you can be blatant about it, you can be polite about it, but everything is political.

In the final analysis, I am tired of pounding the audience, but I still do it, I guess it's in my bloodlines!

Uma: In each play you are motivated by that bane of all idealists, the desire to change the world, and you adopt metaphor and satire as your main tools.

Let us briefly talk about two or three specific plays. I would like to start with your first major play, the one with the colourful title—*Baba Jacques Dass and Turmoil at Cote-des-Neiges Cemetery* (1986). I love the Montreal setting you use. I like the Canadianness of your setting and themes. Universals are okay, but it is the specifics that give life to a piece of contemporary writing. You can see I am trying to shape this interview after my ideology, which is that we should be writing about the here and now.

Rana: It is okay by me because you are one of a few, outside our Serai circle, who understands what I am trying to do.

Uma: *Baba Jacques* is your first play and so you have cast your critical eye on the Indo-Canadian community. But there are other targets as well.

Rana: Yes, the first target was the rule about 'no dirty laundry washing in the public.' The second was about how and why new immigrants were succumbing to the patently patronizing ethno-submersion programme of Canadian multiculturalism.

Uma: That is a difficult balancing act. To deride a minority community on the one hand, and to speak about the majority's oppression of minorities on the other.

Earlier you spoke about your search for precision and your love of spectacle. Two of your most ambitious sets have been in *Five or Six Characters in Search of Toronto* and *The Sulpician Escarpment.* The former has a confounding array of action on the stage, with live music and strobe lights and fluorescent costumes, street signs, etc., but everything worked really well and you pulled it off. In *The Sulpician Escarpment*, you had two brilliant ideas—one of using a Montreal landmark with both historical precision and abstruse symbolism, and the other of having three unrelated men from India stepping off the same plane in Montreal and then tracing interconnections between them. There was so much promise there, the acting was good, there was a measure of suspense and local interest etc. but somehow the play did not succeed. What went wrong? Did stagecraft have something to do with it?

Rana: *Escarpment* was going to be our magnum opus! Yes, that's how I felt. Years of experimentation on stage, on introducing filmic elements (I had shot extensive stock on the railway lines in Calcutta and Montreal and had edited them together), the film-noire angle—cobbled streets, gas lamps, the Dashiell Hammett figures and with the backdrop of exile politics—voila! We had a murder mystery on top of that. I guess the *Escarpment* introduced too many edges. The average theatre-goer, and I do not mean it in a derogatory sense, is not prepared for so many disparate elements. There were times when people were. In fact, my plays would fly in New York city. Montreal is too caught up in its own separatist angst. The other reason why it did not take off was because the intensity of relationships between the two main characters sort of got in the way of the progress of the plot.

Uma: What you have said about your early life has helped me, and will help a great many others, appreciate the nuances of *The Sulpician Escarpment.* All your plays demand a lot of work on the part of the spectator/reader, and I have done my homework, as you and others in the field know. But I confess I throw up my hands when it comes to *The Death of Abbie Hoffman.* William Wordsworth wrote his *Preface to the Lyrical Ballads* to educate his generation into reading poetry the way he did. Please don't be as verbose and repetitive as he was, but could you educate me into seeing what you are getting at?

Rana: I admire Abbie as I have admired Lenny Bruce; I say this because Abbie was a symbol of a time, that is now lost forever, no matter what. It was a time of rebel spirit laced with enormous comic-relief about the contrite ways of the Establishment. The passing of Abbie, his 'death' to me was the defeat of ideology and the birth of the rightwing trash 'common sense' counter revolution. So the larger picture is the ignoble collapse of passionate beliefs in change—that is the death.

But it's all going to come back, in different ways.

Abbie, aside from being written with symbolic disdain for the consensus of triumphant right-ism, is also a reflection of the notion of 'point-counterpoint' theory—which means the sharply divided lines of separation are no longer feasible. With the advent of this much used terminology of 'globalization', there has come a blurring of lines. Revolutionary zeal can become oppressive. The right can make some intrinsic sense. The enemy can sometimes be very rational. Within a big lie, there is a big truth. Or, simply put, learn from the enemy. So in the larger context, this free flow of knowledge highways has had some mixed impact on politics and the emotions. Chaos and lack of roots are not so bad after all.

I think chaos can bring order. So the 'death' has to go from our lives. Abbie, I love him. He was a bend in the road. You know, I got the idea for *Abbie* from Badal Sircar's *Michhil* [Procession] and I kind of readapted it to the nineties. Abbie was a refreshing look at everything, a direct attack on hypocrisy, and his death was symbolic of a passing of an age of youthful challenge. And I trashed the right as well as the boringly correct. So it caused some confusion.There you go!

Uma: I have been writing about *Serai* as part of South Asian Canadian Literature because you are its founder and lead figure, but *Serai* is perhaps to be seen as a voice of the minorities rather than as South Asian Canadian. How do you feel about this?

Rana: Personally, I am a South Asian Canadian. Personally, I will always be an Indian; but I am willing to transform myself into anything else if it would help the cause. But *Serai* the magazine is evolving into the voice of the minority communities, as you said; the guy who does the cover for our magazine is Armenian; Lisa is Irish in origin; the guy who is helping us with the layout is Quebecois; Mark Krupa is a multilingal Canadian born in Montreal of Polish origins; Jaspreet is a Sikh chemical engineer from India, who is completing his Ph.D. here; Prasun Lala, who is in Teesri Duniya's recent play, is a Bengali born here in Montreal, and part of our original group. One of our young writers is David Austin, a black person who grew up in England. Himmat is our musical giant. He is a gay activist with many years in England. And there is Kiran, of mixed Italian and Gujarati descent. There are the stalwarts—Dolores and Nilambri, Anglo-Indian and Punjabi. So there's a good mix of South Asians and other backgrounds. We are a special blend.

Uma: In many ways, Serai, the theatre Serai, is like the theatre you grew up with, passionate but unrecognized, with no money but nevertheless active. However, there are the practical realities of financing a repertory theatre. As you say in *On the Double*, when an Englishman has an emotion, he suppresses it; when a Canadian has an emotion, he applies for government funding. Do you think you might ever get funding from any government or community source?

Rana: I am not saying we want funding from South Asians; nor do we want money from the government because we are minorities; we deserve funding because we provide alternative theatre.

Uma: One last question to bring this talk full circle. Given all the trappings of high tech to which you have access, are you satisfied with yourself vis-a-vis Tapas Sen?

Rana: I will always feel humble before the feats of Tapas Sen in those times. But technically, I believe in zapping the audience—why put them through an hour and a half of entertainment, which they paid for, and let them go without a charge! Therefore, I will always do hi-tech effects. The problem, though, is dineros! Robert Lapage uses electrical hoists, swings, motors, computerized holograms—obviously Serai is still and will be a beggar's opera. But we will give the audience a blast anyway, plus serve thoughts to go home with. The times are bad, Uma. Political content has to be subtextual, but achieved with techno-effects. And form is important. Yes! The medium is the message.

This is a lightly edited version of the interview that appeared in Seagull Theatre Quarterly, *issue no. 19.*